Felipe Alou..

My Life and Baseball

--------------------------- ●

By Felipe Alou

with Herm Weiskopf

WORD BOOKS • WACO, TEXAS

Preface

Felipe Alou was at the wheel of his car driving through the streets of Santo Domingo. As he approached an intersection a car coming from the left did not stop. Alou veered to the right. The driver of the other car pursued him, almost forcing him off the road. Then the driver reached out of his car window in an effort to shake hands. "Felipe! Felipe!" he shouted and then, satisfied, roared away.

As it turned out, this was not an unusual happening in the Dominican Republic, where Felipe is revered. He cannot pass unnoticed. Everyone knows Felipe. They all wave to him as he drives by, or they call out to him or they risk having an accident just so they can shake his hand.

Felipe tolerates this and much more, for he knows the mind of his people and the respect they hold for him. It is difficult for an American to fathom the status Alou enjoys in his homeland because it transcends the hero-worship that is so common in the United States.

When Felipe came to bat for the first time in a practice session before the start of the 1966-67 Dominican League season, hundreds of people at the park stopped their conversation and walked closer to the diamond. There were no cheers when he hit the very first pitch over the left field fence. But when Felipe finished hitting, the crowd as if on cue, turned and many of the fans left the park. They had come to see Felipe. They were satisfied.

Alou's status is perhaps best described by Thimo Pimental, a sports writer for ¡Ahora!, a leading magazine in the Dominican Republic. "The people," Pimental says, "feel that Felipe can do no wrong. When he gets involved in a controversy it is usually because he is standing up for the rights of others. People were disappointed when he stopped playing ball last winter [in the winter of 1965-66 Alou dropped out of the Dominican League because officials were flaunting rules]. But the people knew that Felipe was right. They respect him for his high moral standards and that's unique when a ballplayer reaches such a position. Everybody loves Felipe."

It is hard not to like Felipe, a man of obvious physical strength who so often is so tender. His willingness to help others, his compassion, his sincerity and his ready smile have endeared him to many people. One of the truly great pleasures of my life has been working on this book with Felipe Alou.

HERM WEISKOPF.

Acknowledgments

In writing this book it quickly became apparent that help was needed and a "thank you" here is only a small token of how sincerely I appreciate the aid that so many people willingly gave. There were, at *Sports Illustrated* alone, eight who were most helpful: Andre Laguerre, Jack Tibby, Betty DeMeester, George Bloodgood, Jack Olsen, Ted Stephney, Mort Sharnik, and, above all, Les Woodcock.

Invaluable statistical help was provided by Seymour Siwoff and Bernie Levy of the Elias Sports Bureau, Inc. Also lending a hand were three members of the Atlanta Braves' staff—Donald Davidson, travelling secretary; Jerald Sachs, public relations director; and Lee Walburn, director of press relations.

Reverend Hubert Cook and Reverend and Mrs. Jack Hawthorne also pitched in. As one crisis seemed to pile atop another, there came help from the Lawrences—John and Jean—and from Bob Genberg. Lee Allen, historian for the baseball Hall of Fame, came up with the answers to numerous questions. There was advice from Watson Spoelstra and the constant assistance of Mrs. Mabel Frueh, both invaluable. Jarrell McCracken, president of Word Books, and George Baskin, director of Word Books, displayed much-needed longsuffering and patience.

Even my daughters—LeeAnn, Lydia and Dawn—were there when needed to empty the many waste baskets filled with crumpled pages. And there was my wife JoAnn, ever ready with encouragement and lots of hot coffee.

To all, my most heartfelt thanks.

HERM WEISKOPF.

Contents

To
JoAnn and Maria

CHAPTER 1

THE SLEEPING CAT

Sunday, October 2, 1966, was a day I had been looking forward to for a long time. It was the day that the baseball season would end and it was, above all, the day that I could return to my home in the Dominican Republic. This was my 11th year as a professional baseball player, 11 years of being away from my homeland for seven months at a time. When the final game of the season ended in Cincinnati, I said goodbye to my teammates on the Atlanta Braves and was on my way home. Or so I thought.

Hurricane Inez intervened. Inez, with her swirling, devastating winds of up to 160 miles an hour, had changed course and was headed for Miami. My plane from Cincinnati put down in Tampa, Florida. Nobody knew when we would take off again. It was impossible to get a telephone call through to the Dominican Republic. There was nothing to do but wait. Sunday night turned into Monday morning, and Monday into Tuesday. Finally, on the morning of Wednesday, October 5th, the weather cleared and I boarded a plane heading for Santo Domingo. When we touched down a few hours later at the Pan American field, I could see that Inez, one of the worst storms to batter the Caribbean in years, had been comparatively kind to the Dominican Republic. Its full fury had been felt, though, just across the border in Haiti.

At home that night with my family, I sat and enjoyed the warm breeze that came through the open door. It is very easy to just sit and think in my country. This is the land I love most, the land I come home to when the major league baseball season is over. Thanks to my career in baseball, I am able to live comfortably both in the United States during the season and in the Dominican Republic during the offseason.

Still, I enjoy going back to look at the little house where I grew up in the town of Haina on the southern coast of our island nation. As always, the house wears the same colors it has worn since it was first built—blue with light red trimming. Strange colors? Perhaps they are to some people. To me, though, they have always seemed warm, pleasant. Many a friend from another country has looked at that home I grew up in and has asked much the same question, "How could eight people, including three big league ballplayers, have lived in that tiny place?" As I look at the house, which measures slightly less than 15 feet by 15 feet, I sometimes have to ask myself the same question.

My father built the house in 1934 and a year later, on May 12, I was born in the living room of our home, with a midwife providing the only assistance my mother had during my howling entrance into the world. In later years there came three brothers and two sisters—in order, they were Maria, Mateo, Jesus, Juan and Virginia. It made for a full house, especially since there were just four rooms, yet we managed to live happily in our snuggled-up quarters.

My father, who worked as a carpenter-blacksmith, built almost every piece of furniture we had in our house—the wooden chairs, the large dining room table and the sturdy crib, which I was the first to make use of and which my brothers and sisters also had for their first bed. When we grew older, my father built regular beds for us. I use the term "regular beds" somewhat loosely. What he did was to build solid wood bedframes and slats. Over the slats he placed wire strands which had been gathered from the debris at various construction sites. Stray pieces of cloth and goat skins, if we had any, were placed on top of the wires to make our mattresses. Because our rooms were so small, we had to cram as many people into a bed as possible and as our family grew in number it became necessary to abandon our doubling up policy and to begin tripling up. For a few years I had to share the same bed with Matty and Maria. Cramped living didn't bother us too much because this was the way our neighbors had to live also. We somehow managed to get along with this relatively primitive furniture, and didn't even miss things like innerspring mattresses, plush carpeting, fancy coffee tables, refrigerators, washing machines, a good set of chinaware or even a television set.

Our kitchen was separate from the rest of the house, about 15 feet outside the dining room door. Actually, it was nothing more than three large rocks with a fire built between them. It's surprising the good food my mother turned out here. She would use palm leaves to cover the pots so that the rain or dirt could not get in our food.

The menu was monotonous but good. For breakfast we always had strong black coffee—and bread, very dark and very filling. Even when we were two or three years old we drank coffee, mainly because it was plentiful and cheap. Our big meal of the day was at noon. Rice, red beans and fish were almost always on the table. To this day, if I don't eat rice at least once a day I just don't feel that I have eaten. At about 6 o'clock in the evening we would eat supper. This meal often consisted of boiled plantain, which is an oversized variety of

2

banana. Mother would boil our plantain in water. (They're better fried in peanut oil—but she saved a penny or so by boiling them . . . and every penny counted in those days.) Along with plantain came some more fish (broiled or fried) and usually a glass of milk from our flock of goats, a flock that one time numbered as high as 13.

Dad, whom I called Abundio, was a great fisherman. I thought nothing of getting up at 3 o'clock in the morning so that I could go with him to catch the fish for the day's meals. It was only a mile or so down to the Caribbean Sea, depending on which spot on the rocks we were going to fish from. If the moon had gone down, Abundio would make a torch from a piece of automobile tire (part of the treasure found alongside the road). Our bamboo pole, cut out of the nearby jungle, held a strand of construction wire in place of regulation fishing line. This was the same wire that we used in making our mattresses, so that we could just climb into bed and pull out some fishing line.

Bait was crabs, sardines, or shrimp from the Haina River, about a mile in the other direction from our house. Mostly we caught groupers and snappers. Sometimes we would even come home with a few lobsters.

As jagged as the rocks along the Caribbean coastline were, we never minded clambering around them barefoot; going barefoot was a way of life. One of the first lessons we learned was that we each had only one pair of shoes, and that they must be carefully polished and saved for school and church.

Dad wasn't able to work out plumbing for our home, so we had to make frequent trips to the river to keep a supply of water. We had to make two trips a day. The first one usually came early . . . between 3 and 5 o'clock in the morning so that we could get to the river while the water was still clean. Each of us would take two buckets down to the river and then wade waistdeep into the cool water where we could get the buckets brimful with just one scoop. We would then walk the mile back to the house carrying one bucket of water by hand and the other on top of our head. Fresh water was kept in the dining room, in a sort of tub made out of mud. It kept the water nice and cool for hours.

The river served for washing ourselves and our clothing, as well as for fresh water and fishing bait. Doing the wash was always something to be looked forward to, for there were always plenty of other kids at the river and we were all permitted to splash around in the water as much as we wanted to.

I look back now and see that Father, who gained great respect as a builder of most of the homes in Haina, was much too easygoing to ever make much money from his carpentering. He did some work in a

3

small shop behind the house, but most of his jobs were away from home. Lots of times he would leave early on a Monday morning, his horse laden with his tools, to build a house for someone. On Saturday night, if we were not already in bed, we would watch for him to return so that we could run out to greet him. He was, and still is, a quiet man, yet when he saw all his kids running to welcome him he would sing out and then he'd pick up the smaller children and whirl them around. Those were homecomings worth remembering.

I remember one very sad homecoming. Sometimes dad would go off to help build a factory. These trips would keep him away from us for three weeks at a time. Once, after such a trip, he returned late on a Saturday night. He had been given a ride home by one of the other workmen, who let him out of the car on the highway near our house. Workmen had been repairing a drain along the highway. Dad could see that there was some sort of a hole—but the hole was a good bit bigger than he thought—and when he tried to jump over it he fell right in. We were all in bed already. Dad had hurt himself pretty badly, but managed to get out by yelling for help until someone heard him and came to get him out. He had to be taken to the hospital, there to spend more than a week in traction while his injured back mended.

There were other homecomings that were not happy ones. Sometimes dad would break the news to Mom that, well, those people he had worked for all week didn't have much money. Maybe they gave him $2, maybe $3. They always promised to pay him "someday soon." That sort of installment-plan financing was all right if you were a large business and had a bank account to fall back on. For Jose and Virginia Alou and their six children, however, there was no such thing as a bank account. In my country there is a saying about the type of kitchen that we had. It goes like this: "When you can see the cat sleeping between the rocks, then you know there is no food in the house." I saw the cat sleeping between the rocks more times than I like to recall.

Money was always scarce. But one day my father was a little ahead. His employers had paid him on time, and he had a $10 bill and a $1 bill. (American money was the official currency until shortly after World War II.) One of those vendors who travels through the hills selling vegetables and fruit came to our house. Dad picked out some tomatoes and green vegetables and handed the woman the $10 bill. She gave him change for a $1 bill, then left. A little later Dad started looking for that $10 bill. He couldn't find it. Everybody started crying. I was just old enough to realize the utter tragedy of his mistake.

4

It was on nights such as this that the sounds of the Caribbean had a deeper-than-usual meaning, almost as though the rush of the waves had a voice that was able to communicate with each of us. From our back door we could see the ocean, see the endless waves chase each other to nowhere, then crash and slip away again; large and powerful one moment, dissipated the next. There were lessons that could be learned from the sea. One that helped me was the thought that no matter what the situation is at present, no matter how bleak things look, life goes on. Our house was well situated for learning basic lessons from nature. On the other side of the house we could look up into the rugged Central Mountains, which begin to rise about two miles to the north.

Losing that $10 bill was not the worst thing that ever happened to us. There were times during the war when there was very, very little food to be had. It was during those years that we had to do without many other things, too. Kerosene, for instance. We only had one lamp at our house. We kept the lamp in the living room at night and if anyone had to go to another room, he had to take the lamp along. When we couldn't afford kerosene, or it was unavailable, we used the same kind of torch we did for fishing—a strip from an automobile tire. I'm sure you've smelled burning rubber. Just imagine how much of an odor there was in our living room! Well, the odor may have been bad, and smoke may have made our eyes water, but we felt that it was better to sit and talk in the smelly, smokey half-dark than it was to sit in total blackness. Matches were imported, so were unavailable during those war years. Candles were scarce and much too expensive for us. Without matches, we had to get a fire started and keep it going. It was my job, before I went to bed, to remember to bed the fire with slow-burning wood.

As I said before, money was almost non-existent in those days. My father's little carpenter and blacksmith shop almost went broke, for nobody could afford to have even the smallest jobs done. We couldn't buy things from the *colmado,* or small grocery store, which was about 150 yards from the house. More than ever, we had to rely on fish from the Caribbean and fruit from the trees in our backyard—grapefruit, coconuts and oranges. Sometimes we were able to sell some of the coconuts. This helped our cash supply a little—but I liked the coconut trees for another reason. When they were too tall for us to knock the coconuts down with a long, hooked pole, I would just climb up the trunk.

I climbed a lot of coconut trees when I was a boy. By the time I got 20 or 25 feet up, I was usually in a world of my own: on watch in the crow's nest of a ship far at sea, or standing proudly atop a mountain that I had just conquered. Invariably someone below would remind me that my real mission was to knock the coconuts out of the tree, not to sight pirate vessels or to scale the Matterhorn.

I didn't worry about falling out of the tree. It was more dangerous for those on the ground. One day a coconut fell right on my mother's arm. It probably broke her arm, for she still has trouble with it. In those days, though, there was no way we could have had it X-rayed, and the local doctor's skills were limited.

Matty could have ended his baseball career before he got started good, for when he fell out of a mango tree we had the same problem finding a good doctor. Somewhere we had heard of Tarzan, king of the jungle. Matty was about eight years old. Tarzan impressed him greatly, so that he began practicing swinging from limb to limb in the mango trees. One day he swung, missed, and landed on his left arm. It hung real funny, at an angle, like it was dislocated. It seemed to me that all the doctor did was to massage it a little, very briefly, and ask for his fee. This was one of the times we had no money, and this was all right with the doctor, for what he really wanted was merchandise. The prize of our small barnyard was a fighting cock named La Ley, The Law. He wasn't too much to look at, but he had earned some money for us and had never been defeated in 10 fights. And the doctor wanted him. There was no way out. It took a long time for us to walk back home to get La Ley, but it took much longer to walk back to the doctor's little office with La Ley's inquisitive head poking out from under my shirt.

There's no place for cock fighting in the States. But at that time in our country it was an accepted form of recreation and a highly regarded sporting event. Almost everyone kept roosters, or wished they could. I had a rooster of my own in those days and used to squander every penny I could get away with to buy grain for him. He had the makings of a big winner. I took him out every time I had a chance. There was no question of training him . . . he just loved to fight. He had won two matches at the time he tangled with an opponent out of his class. He was run over by a pickup truck in front of our house. I should have kept him penned up, I guess, but all the chickens in our neighborhood ranged far and wide. I wanted to bury him with proper honors, but he had too much meat on his bones to let him go to waste. Instead of a funeral, he was given a roasting and served for dinner that day. I took one look at the remains of my once-proud, once-honored rooster, began to cry and left the table without eating a bite.

As scarce as food always seemed to be, there were times when it literally walked right into our kitchen. In May and June, when the heavy rains would swell the Haina River over its banks, that fruitful river would deposit crabs all over the landscape. They were everywhere—in the yard, in the road—and it was not uncommon for us to get up in the morning and find a dozen crabs waiting for us in the kitchen, a very functional and tasty turn of events.

During those months, the caves along the river were filled with water and the crabs thought them an ideal place to set up housekeeping. Their living habits did not escape us, and together with Matty and Jesus I used to go down to the caves to get some for supper. Sometimes they got us. Many, many times I had my fingers bitten, and there is still in my mind a vivid picture of a frightened Matty running home, yelling all the way, with a huge crab hanging from his arm.

But a good many times I, too, got more than I bargained for. Once I helped myself to some of my father's fishing gear and sneaked down to the ocean with a friend. I caught a four-pound grouper that afternoon, a feat that caused more alarm than delight in my pounding heart; to take it home would be inviting a spanking. Yet we couldn't just throw away such a prize. One infraction of the rules tends to lead to another and in our case we compounded our first misdemeanor by going to my grandmother's house and helping ourselves to some of her pans and matches. Then, with pans, matches, grouper and poles in hand, we ducked into the woods, built a fire, cooked and consumed as much of the fish as our stomachs could hold. We got through the whole incident without being caught by anyone, but at dinner that night I could hardly eat anything and I found it hard to look my parents in the eye and tell them I wasn't hungry.

Taking my dad's fishing equipment was a cardinal sin. He also became angry when we would go down to the caves for crabs or when we would go swimming in the ocean, two fairly dangerous pastimes that we persisted in taking part in. When he found us guilty of such behavior, my dad, upset because his words of caution had not penetrated our stubborn heads, applied a more convincing form of logic to a more vulnerable portion of our anatomy. My father was a powerful man and was an exceptionally fast runner. There were times when Matty and Jesus would try to run away from him to avoid a licking. They never succeeded. Oh yes, I tried to avoid my punishment in this way and once, when I was 15 and felt as swift as a jungle cat, my father ran me down.

Another thing that got us into trouble with our parents was our trips down to the local sand mine. I went there only once in a while, but Matty used to get a big kick out of fooling around at the sand mine and went there as often as he could. We used to help load the trucks with sand and would then ride on top of the sand piled in the back of the trucks. By discreetly jumping off the trucks before they got too close to our home, we managed to keep our folks from finding out anything about this phase of our activities for the longest time. One day, however, Matty literally got carried away. He was enjoying his ride aboard the truck so much one afternoon that he rode right past our house, through Haina and all the way to Santo Domingo. My parents found out what had happened and when Matty arrived home he got a very warm reception, a little too warm as far as Matty was concerned and for the next few days he had to sit down very gently.

Jesus, I believe got more spankings than the rest of us, largely because he had such a quick temper and because he could not resist sneaking into the kitchen or dining room and helping himself to some food before mealtime. Despite this continual hunger for food, Jesus was skinny until he was about 15. Evidently, though, his eating habits paid off in the long run, for he is now 6 foot 2 and weighs close to 200 pounds.

During those infrequent periods when we managed to stay in my father's good graces, he would sometimes treat us to a ride in a cart he had made. He would hitch up a horse to the cart and away we would go, covering the seven miles to the closest part of Santo Domingo in an hour and a half. It was not until years later that we had a car in our family. Matty bought an old English car, a relic which, when he was able to keep it running, brought us spasms of happiness hitherto unknown. When he first brought that car home we all piled into it and went for a ride. It was not quite the same as riding down Broadway in a Cadillac, but it brought us a measure of joy and pride we had never been accustomed to.

Money, food and transportation were ours in only the most limited degree during those growing-up years, yet our troubles were no different than those of many people and they were certainly less than those of many others. For one thing, we always had a roof over our heads, and that was more than some of our neighbors could say after one of the hurricanes struck our area. More than once I saw the roof of someone's house take flight. When the storm ended, I would go outside to gape at the strange-looking houses, standing there—the four walls erect, the roof gone—like plucked roosters.

Our home survived all storms, largely because my father had used the best materials he could afford. Unlike most of the homes in our region, which had dirt floors, we had a cement floor. Since our house was sturdier than most, many people would use our home as a shelter when storms came.

In those days there were no warnings about impending hurricanes such as there are today. People are now cautioned days in advance about hurricanes with pretty names. No matter what they are called and no matter how much warning there is, though, nothing can take away the fury of the wind. We hadn't been devastated by a hurricane in years, until Inez blew into town, all of which makes the older folks talk even more dramatically about the worst one that every struck the Dominican Republic. That was on September 3, 1930, the day after Trujillo took over power in our country. Two thousand Dominicans lost their lives in that storm, buildings were dismembered and blown away like so much chaff.

After the countryside was cleaned up, the dazed people, with Trujillo spurring them on, embarked on a rebuilding program the likes of which our nation had never before known. Every major highway, hospital and school that we have was built under Trujillo, a dedicated, energetic, dictatorial president who ruled the land for the next three decades. He felt it only fitting that the capital city of Santo Domingo be renamed Ciudad Trujillo in his honor, and whatever Generalissimo Rafael Leonidas Trujillo Molina wanted, Generalissimo Rafael Leonidas Trujillo Molina got.

Under his direction, work began on a world's fair to be held in Santo Domingo—some of us never did appreciate the new name—in 1955. When it became evident that work was lagging and that the fair would not open on schedule, Trujillo gave himself the authority to go out and get whatever manpower he needed to complete the project on time.

One day a few army trucks, under Trujillo's orders, were sent to pick up any man they saw who was not working. I was playing catch in front of the house with Matty when one of the trucks came by. It stopped and a soldier grabbed Matty. I took off, heading for the ocean as fast as I could run. My father was told where Matty was to be taken and then the truck pulled away. Matty was given the privilege of laboring all day at the fairgrounds, a hard day's work for which he didn't earn a penny. The soldiers who had taken Matty away didn't return him, so he had to walk about eight miles to get home that night.

During the summers, from the time I was 8 till I was 11, I used to work on a farm about 30 miles east of Santo Domingo where an uncle of mine was the caretaker. Sometimes I had to get out of bed at midnight to help milk the cows, then bring the milk back to the farmhouse and prepare it for shipment to Santo Domingo. On nights such as this, I was allowed to crawl back into bed at about 4 a.m. and then get up three or four hours later to take care of other chores around the farm. I always enjoyed working on the farm. Although it

9

was a job without pay, it was fun and there was plenty of good fishing in the area, as well as woods I could roam through with my makeshift slingshot. As hard as I tried, I was never as accomplished a marksman with a slingshot as Matty was. He could seemingly cut any V-shaped twig, attach a piece of rubber from an old tire innertube and then go out and hit just about anything he aimed at, including birds on the wing.

In the summer of 1953, when I was 18, I worked at the concrete factory, which was located half a mile from our house. I was paid according to how much I produced and my pay was generally between $9 and $9.50 a week for some of the hardest labor I have ever done. There were just two of us who could stand the heavy work of lugging huge rocks and dumping them into a machine that pulverized them. That machine never got tired, but we did. I worked the night shift, from 7 in the evening until 6 in the morning. Some of the rocks were so big that it took two of us to lift them and feed them into the mouth of this gluttonous rock-crusher. I nicknamed the machine Korea because everyone wanted to stay just as far away from that machine as they wanted to stay away from combat in Korea.

That summer the factory decided to start marketing a line of ready-mix products. Inspectors were on hand to make frequent checks to be certain that the rocks were kept extra clean for this new type of production. I remember that one night one of the workmen had been eating some mangoes and had thrown the skins and pits right on top of the rocks that had just been cleaned. When the inspector came along that night, he saw the mess and let out a howl. He happened to spot me first and began chewing me out.

"How can you do this?" he shouted at me. "You're going to disgrace our business and our name."

I was weary and sleepy-eyed and I snapped back at the inspector, demanding to know where he got the notion that I had made the mess. Normally, no one would ever dare to talk back to one of the inspectors and he wasn't about to take any guff from me. He went right to the foreman of the crew I was working for and told him to fire me at once. I was in luck, though: the foreman was my father. Or was I in luck? When my father found out who the inspector wanted to have fired, he was all set to get rid of me without a moment's hesitation. In a strange turn of affairs during the next few bewildering minutes, it was the inspector—who had just found out that we were father and son—who wound up defending me.

"No," said my father when the inspector tried to protect me. "I'm going to fire him."

When I was finally given a chance to explain that I had not thrown

10

the remains of the mangoes on the clean rocks, everyone seemed pleased and I was allowed to keep my job. After picking up a rock and throwing it into "Korea," however, I got the feeling that maybe I would have been better off had I been fired.

I returned to work at the concrete factory the following summer during my vacation from school. By that time I had begun to establish myself as a baseball player of some merit and I was happy to note that my pay went up ($48 a month) even though my work was cut down. Being a ballplayer in the Dominican Republic brings many fringe benefits.

That was the summer that I became involved in an incident which should have resulted in my being fired, no questions asked. I had been given a much softer job and was allowed to spend a considerable part of my time merely throwing stones at various targets of my own choosing outside the factory. The theory behind this was that all this throwing would strengthen my arm for the baseball season. Everything was quiet and uneventful until the day that my aim was not so good and I put a stone right through the windshield of one of the company trucks. There seemed to be no way out of this jam, for several other people had seen what I had done. We all waited anxiously for the driver of the truck to show up. My fate, and very possibly my job, was in his hands. When he found out that I was the one who had done the damage, he said, "Some day maybe he'll be playing for Escogido [Escogido was one of the two big baseball teams in Santo Domingo and the president of the club was also the owner of the concrete factory] so let's just forget about the whole matter."

That was a break for me, for my family was still very poor and my wages were needed at home. Every penny in hand meant that much more food in the belly. Happily, it has been years since I last saw the cat sleeping in the kitchen.

CHAPTER 2

LEMONS AND FLOUR SACKS

One of the most difficult things for me to get accustomed to in the big leagues has been the strange hours and the lack of regularity that are now so much a part of the game. There is much more to baseball than simply playing the game; that is the most enjoyable part of it. What makes it a grind are the flights that get in at 5 in the morning, the constant bother of being transported from one time zone to another, the problem of trying to get dinner at 2 a.m. after an extra-inning night game. This makes it difficult to get regular sleep.

When the phone keeps ringing, when autograph hounds come at us from every corner, when the team is not going well, when our flight doesn't get in until the wee hours of the morning—it is at these times that I occasionally have to stop and remind myself how fortunate I really am. All I have to do is to think back to the days when I first began playing a crude form of baseball in the Dominican Republic. Had Abner Doubleday seen the sort of baseball we played, he might well have given up the game and taken up quoits. Rarely did we have the luxury of a baseball to play with. Instead, we used lemons. They were green and sort of sweet and, most important, they were plentiful around Haina. They also broke easily when we hit them with our hands, which we used in place of bats. Instead of four bases, we had two and they were usually made of rock, not the foam rubber that even the Little Leaguers have today. We knew very little about the game, but we enjoyed it and it helped while away the long hours. Back home the summer sun gets up at about 5:00 a.m., and so do many of the people; it gets too hot too fast to do much sleeping after that hour. So there were many hours to play.

The problem was that there weren't enough boys around to make up two teams. Our nearest neighbor in those days lived in a little house about 100 yards away, and that was fairly close, because most of the houses were much farther apart. I doubt that the total population of Haina in the early 1940s was more than 2,000.

Dad, seeing our growing interest in baseball, and glad to see that here was something that could channel our energies and keep us out of trouble, started making bats for us in his shop. Before long, he was making them for the other kids in the neighborhood. They weren't

12

Louisville Sluggers, but they gave us the feeling that we were actually playing the game.

Baseballs were harder to come by. For years we used all sorts of make-shifts, and I must have been close to 12 years old before I had my first real baseball . . . one that I found in a field. Several of us had gone to see a local orphanage team play a club from Santo Domingo. The game was played on a diamond which had been set up on a cow pasture. The area around the field was covered with dense underbrush. That day a ball was hit into the scrub country, and some of the fans spent hours searching for it, but never did find it. The next day Matty and I went back. We rooted around in the weeds and bushes for almost an hour before we finally found the ball. Things were looking up! We finally had a real baseball to go with our home-produced bats.

Not until years later did we achieve the sophistication of playing with gloves, too.

Baseball had been highly popular in the Dominican Republic during the early 1930s, and maintained real interest until diplomatic tensions arose with Cuba about 1937. Interest in the game had slowly faded, so that by the time I was in the first or second grade just about the only baseball that was played was that on the school ground. And even that was poorly supervised and poorly equipped.

The first school I ever attended was in Haina, a small, crowded wooden building, traditional red in color, with all three grades crammed into the one room. Teaching at the school frequently was a community affair, with some of the wiser adults filling in when the regular teacher was too ill or too indifferent to show up—or sometimes when there simply wasn't any teacher available. I'm so proud that it's no longer that way. Haina has a first-rate school, and the teachers are well-trained and conscientious.

Fist fights were a part of the basic curriculum, or at least were the number one extra-curricular activity at our little school. But I didn't like to fight. I recall that when I was six years old the older boys used to taunt me by saying that I was afraid to fight, that I was a sissy. Despite the fact that I was big and strong for my age, I just didn't like to fight. It wasn't that I was scared. More than anything, I suppose, I was simply a pacifist. This made it easy for me to mind the constant advice of Mom and Dad not to get into schoolyard scraps. Finally, the constant teasing got to the point where the other kids were convinced that I wouldn't fight, no matter what they did or said. One of the boys, a good sized veteran of many a fight, slugged me. He knew I wouldn't fight back.

Well, I doubt that I ever would have done anything about it if my cousin hadn't kept after me, reminding me that Dad and the family couldn't be proud of me if they knew that I had let someone hit me. So I did what I had to do. I fought that boy, and whipped him good. When we got through, I could tell that he had a new and lasting respect for me. Better than that, nobody taunted me anymore, and nobody took any more pokes at me. And even to this day I've never found it necessary to take a swing at anyone else.

After finishing my three years at the little red schoolhouse, I was accepted as an outside student at the orphanage school and attended there for the next three years.

After that, because there wasn't a high school in Haina, I had to move to Santo Domingo and live with an uncle in order to attend school. Uncle Juan was a captain in the army. Under Trujillo, who tried to keep his officers on his side by paying them handsomely, he earned a good salary, so he was able to give me board and lodging. I helped him and my aunt around the house whenever I could. They were really good to me, and even gave me bus fare so I could go home to Haina on Friday, be with my family all weekend, and return on Monday for another week of schooling. Two years of this was more than enough, and when I was 17 I decided that I was big enough to make the trip from home (in Haina) to the school (in Santo Domingo) each day on foot. The main drawback was that this was a 12 mile trip each way. I had hopes of getting a ride at least part of the way, for with the building of a gigantic sugar mill in Haina the traffic between the two cities became much heavier, and many of the drivers didn't mind picking up students.

Still, to get to school on time, I had to get up at 5 o'clock in the morning. After a breakfast of black coffee and bread, I would get out to the road and try to hitch a ride on one of the early trucks making a run to Santo Domingo. Most of the roads in the Dominican Republic at that time were not too good, but this one at least was paved enough to let the drivers drive at moderate speeds. Between walking and riding like that I was never once late for a day of school, even though on some mornings I failed to get a ride and had to walk the full 12 miles. Sometimes now when I pay a visit to that high school, students tell me that teachers still hold me up as an example for getting to class on time.

All this walking was good for my legs, and this was good for baseball. I was beginning to establish myself as a baseball player, and had concentrated on this sport to the exclusion of everything else. But I hung around all kinds of sports, and began to watch the track and field events pretty carefully. I hesitated to try out for anything until one day a group of us were down on the field watching our best javelin thrower. He made some good throws, and some that were only

fair, and we began kidding each other saying that we could throw
farther than that. Well, I must have talked loudest, for the coach overheard me and really put me on the spot by saying, "Why don't you
come out and try it right now?" There was no way of backing out, so
I picked up a javelin and started throwing it, not too artfully and not
too far. But the coach had seen me play baseball, and knew that I at
least had a strong arm. He urged me to start working out with the
team.

I'll never forget that when I went to my first class after that
impromptu trial the teacher, a delicate lady named Mrs. Furet, took
one look at my sweaty clothes and ordered me out of her room. When
the coach came to appeal on my behalf and to say that it was his
fault that I was so grimy, she ordered him out of the room, too, and
told him that if he wanted me on his team he should give me a team
uniform. The coach gave me a uniform at once.

We practiced after school, and often would work out so late that I
couldn't make the trip home and still have time left for studying. I'd
spend the night with Uncle Juan or at the home of one of my friends
so I could sleep a little later in the morning and wouldn't have to
worry about walking 12 miles to get to school.

In addition to throwing the javelin, I ran in the 100- and 200-meter
dashes. I thought I was a pretty fast runner, for my times in the
dashes were excellent by local standards. But one day when I looked
at the world records I discovered I was just mediocre. What speed I
had was natural, and there was never enough coaching to help refine
it, to eliminate flaws, or to teach me those small details that can be so
vital in the short races. I was pleased with the progress I made in
throwing the javelin. I definitely needed coaching there, also, but when
I was 19, and a senior, I threw 204 feet. That throw is still a record
in my homeland.

That was the year—my senior year in high school—when I went to
the Central American Games in Mexico City to represent my country
in the dash events, plus the discus and javelin. I probably should have
stayed home. The javelin was my best event, and there I finished fifth.
It was a bad year for us all around. The Dominican baseball team
had finished far down in the standings. I remember that the manager
of the club spoke to me after the Games. "Felipe," he said, "we need
a catcher for next year at the Pan American Games. If you go home
and practice, I think you could come back next year as our catcher."
This helped to dull the disappointment of showing up so poorly in
the Games, and I guess helped to set me on the road to baseball
rather than track and field.

When I got home from Mexico City, I took his advice and began working out behind the plate. But I didn't like catching. I like to run. I like the freedom of moving around, and going after the ball that's hit a long way from me. So I returned to the outfield.

I should explain that although track and field had pulled me right out of high school baseball, I had continued to play in other leagues during the summer. When I was 16 I started playing for a team called La Fe, in Santo Domingo. The games were played at night, and believe it or not, there was a league rule against hitting a home run. It was a pitcher's dream.

What made this situation possible was that all the league games were played on a softball field, with short fences. To counteract this, the rule stated that "over the fence is a double."

Although I was, and still am, proud of our team, La Fe was a rinkydink outfit. We might have finished last in the standings, but we dazzled 'em with our uniforms made out of flour sacks—white with red stripes down the legs.

Interest in baseball was growing. Actually, I think what brought baseball back to prominence in the Dominican Republic was the Brooklyn Dodgers, of all things. I mentioned before that baseball seemed to be dying after the Cuban players couldn't play in our country anymore. Probably the war had a lot to do with it, too. But that was before the Dodgers set up their spring training camp in 1948, in Santo Domingo. Baseball has never been the same since. Neither have I. I practiced my first curve, with a lemon, after hearing the radio announcer talking about those Dodger pitchers throwing curves. To my amazement, we could actually see that lemon move in or out.

Even in 1948 we couldn't afford a radio. There was one in a grocery store, and we would walk the mile down there in a group, swapping jokes and baseball stories, to hear the game. People came from all over that section of the country to listen to those Dodger games.

Bigger than the thrill of throwing my first curve was seeing the Dodgers play a team of Dominican All-Stars. All of our patriotic fervor was aroused during these games. I remember one game when it looked like our club could actually defeat this major league team from the States. Going into the ninth inning, the Dominicans led 3-2. It seemed too good to be true. It was. Brooklyn Pitcher Paul Minner hit a two-run homer in the ninth to give the Dodgers a 4-3 victory.

So, the Dodgers did a great deal to forward the cause of baseball in my country, and by the time I began playing with the La Fe team we had no trouble getting a team together or attracting a crowd to watch us play. Even the problem of equipment had eased up a little bit. Little by little we had outfitted our team, but the greatest step had come when my father somehow managed to scrape up enough money to buy me my first pair of baseball spikes from a pawn shop. I was proud of them. I did everything but wear them to bed, and one night I even walked the 12 miles from the ball park to Haina wearing those spikes.

Those 12 miles from home to the ball park may have been the reason for a big disappointment. Twelve miles meant the difference to me between being a city boy and a country boy. And my closest rival for the batting championship was a city boy. Some of the city boys thought I was a country hick, even though I was going to school in Santo Domingo. But all the batting averages were kept by a city boy . . . sort of informally, as it turned out. After our final game of the season during one of the years when I was playing with La Fe the league statistician came to me and asked me what my batting average was. I told him that I wasn't positive of the exact figure but that I was certain that I had hit at least .500. When the final league batting averages were released, my average was listed at .394. Somehow, with having played another game, my average had dropped 100 or more points. Worse yet, another player was credited with a .400 average, good enough to beat me out for the title by six points.

Following that season, I moved up to a tougher league, where they had a prize for being the leading hitter—a new fielder's glove. I was determined to win that glove, and tried as hard as I could. I just couldn't do it! The same player who edged me out in the other league finished ahead of me again. How he accomplished this is still a mystery to me. He must have hit close to 1.000. My batting average, I know, was about .800. Some of my friends still tell me that I was robbed both times.

Time takes care of disappointments like this, of course, and the years have taken away some of the sting, but I can still recall how much I wanted that glove. It was over a year later that Uncle Juan bought me a brand new one. It was the first baseball glove that I had ever owned. Up until that time I had always had to borrow gloves from other boys. This glove therefore meant a lot to me, and I took loving care of it. As it turned out, that was a mistake. A day or two after I got the glove I rubbed it down with coconut oil to preserve its flexibility and good looks. The next time I went out to practice I discovered it had a good bit more flexibility than was desirable, for the oil had attracted rats who chewed about 50 holes in it. All those holes didn't keep me from playing with my precious glove, though, even if it was extra-well ventilated, and I used it for the next few years.

CHAPTER 3

TWO YEARS
OF DECISION

Time for college. Behind me were the graduation exercises, the pride of being a senior, the joy of feeling my mind stretch as I discovered the new worlds of high school science and math and languages. Ahead of me was adulthood, medical school, and all of life. I was already beginning to forget the poverty of my childhood, even though we still lived in the house in Haina that dad had built for his young family. It was unbelievably crowded.

Mother and Dad had very early set their sights on college and careers in the professions for their children. Long ago we had decided that after high school I would take the pre-med course at the University of Santo Domingo, and then study to be a surgeon. Now that road lay directly ahead of me, and the path looked bright and sure. My participation in sports would help me get the education I wanted so badly.

I had already worked out some with the University baseball team, so when plans were being made for the team to go on a trip to the States, the coach asked me to go along as part of the team. We were scheduled to play games against such college squads as Colgate, Yale, Cornell, and Columbia. Technically, I was not yet a student at the University and somebody raised an objection to my making the trip. Although I wanted to play with the team, and had looked forward to the trip, I actually was somewhat relieved when it was decided that I should not be allowed to go. If I had gone one of the other players who had been playing regularly for the University would have been left behind.

A few months later, though, I was officially a member of the team. I had enrolled for my pre-med course, and was engrossed in studies and baseball. The coach installed me as the cleanup hitter and I was fortunate enough to get 11 hits in my first 11 times up in collegiate competition. Ours was a fine team. We won the collegiate championship and earned the right to participate in the annual amateur tournament, which is the highlight of baseball activity in the Dominican Republic. Each year, starting on March 24th, teams throughout the country begin competition for the right to get into this tournament. It is a short season, terminating at the end of June, and teams play only

18

on weekends — one game on Saturday and a doubleheader every Sunday.

Our team got off to a good start in that 1955 tournament, winning the sectional title and advancing to a playoff against a team from Santiago to determine which club would move into the final round. It was my first visit to Santiago and a memorable one. Santiago: our second largest city, tucked away in the northwest corner of the country, some 90 miles and a three-and-a-half-hour bus ride away. We arrived the night before the game, did some sight-seeing and then made the trip a complete success by winning the next day.

During the first round of the tournament I had 26 hits in 35 times at bat, giving me a batting average of .743. My hitting, as well as that of my teammates, dropped off in the championship round against an armed forces team, however. One of the service teams almost always wins the national championship, for they are generally blessed with the most talented players. We were no match for the service team and lost in the final round of the tournament.

When the tournament ended, I devoted my spare time to getting ready for another trip to Mexico City, where I was to compete in the sprint and javelin throwing. For weeks I put in long, arduous hours of practice. Then, the night before the Games got underway, I was taken out of the track and field events and placed on the baseball team. It was a mixed-up affair that revolved around where it would be best to put my talents to use. The final reasoning of the officials was that we had little chance of winning a gold medal in track and field but that we had reason to hope for one in baseball. On the last day of competition I got four hits and we beat the American team 10-8 to earn the gold medal.

Scouts from the Pittsburgh Pirates and Milwaukee Braves took an interest in some of the long home runs I hit during the Pan-American Games. The Pirate scout in particular expressed his interest in me, even though I wasn't the best hitter on our team. There were rumors that the scouts wanted me to turn professional. That was in the days of Trujillo, however, and no scouts were permitted to approach any of our players without first obtaining permission from the team manager. An army major was our manager and he told the scouts in no uncertain terms that they were not to talk to me about signing any contract. He went further, telling them that it would be a good while before I could be a professional athlete because the Dominican Republic track and field coaches were already preparing me for the 1956 Olympic Games in Melbourne.

It was all a bit confusing and once I got back home I talked matters over with my parents. They didn't want me to sign any baseball contract; they had always wanted me to be a doctor. I had wanted to become a doctor. That's why I had started to college. Now that the thought of becoming a professional ballplayer had been implanted in my mind, it caused me some unrest. As appealing and flattering as the notion of playing baseball for a living seemed, though, I resolved that surgeons were more needed than were outfielders.

Other factors soon intervened.

To begin with, almost every other member of our Pan-American club had signed to play professionally in the new Dominican League which was to be launched in October of 1955. Eventually, it reached the point where I was the lone member of the team who had not signed. Each time I heard about another teammate signing, I winced. Baseball had become so much a part of my life in recent years that I was reaching the point where I thought I might want to make it all of my life. Never did I give in to the temptation, as strong as it was; my duty was to family and country and I would become a doctor and I would proudly represent my people in Melbourne. My decision was made. Or, so I thought. Before I knew it, unforeseen events changed the course of my life.

My father lost his job. So did my uncle, who had the audacity to disagree with Trujillo. Suddenly, poverty was no longer a thing of the past; it was imminent and seemed inevitable. After completing almost two years of college, I had to drop out.

And then came a statement from Gomez Oliver, the director of amateur sports in the Dominican Republic. He said that he thought I was ready to play professional baseball. He was interested in me as a member of the Olympic team the following year, but said that as good an athlete as I was, I was never going to be any help to my mother and father as a runner or javelin thrower. Lastly, he said that my parents should grant me permission to sign a contract to play professionally because there was talk that the government, dismayed by the low number of athletes who were capable of competing in the Olympics, was thinking of not sending anyone to Melbourne. My mind, which I thought I had firmly made up by myself, apparently had been made up for me by others and by these latest circumstances.

Next came the decision of which team to sign with. Here, again, my mind was virtually made up for me. Horacio Martinez, my baseball coach at the University of Santo Domingo, had been appointed as a scout for the Giants, who had not yet made their move from New York to San Francisco. He picked up this assignment while on the tour of the United States with his team the year before. Alex Pompez, one of the most successful of all Giant scouts, had seen the team play, had been surprised at the caliber of the players and had told Martinez

20

that if he could find a Dominican who was both talented and willing, he should sign him up for the Giants.

Martinez did precisely that, coming to my home in Haina in December of 1955 with a contract. Reluctantly, my parents consented to my signing. To them it was a disappointment, to them it meant the end of their dream of my becoming a doctor, to them it was sad to think of my going to another country to earn a living. I shared with them their disappointment, their sadness, their anxiety; yet, as I looked at the tired walls of our home, at the crowded rooms, at the weariness in my parents' faces—all accentuated by our crude, flickering little lamp—I could only hope that better days were coming and that I would help bring them.

CHAPTER 4

HELPING HANDS

Before going any further, it is time for me to jump a few years into the future, arriving at June 7, 1958—the most important day of my life. This leapfrogging over the calendar is necessary because what took place that day affects much of what I have to say from here on. Before arriving at June 7, 1958, though, there are some details leading up to that day which must first be brought out.

It all began with a banquet given in my honor after I had returned home from my first season of professional ball. This was quite a big affair and I was a trifle embarrassed by it all. Dozens of my friends were there and they gave me a wide assortment of gifts. The most ridiculous gift was from one of my closest friends, Roque Martinez, who gave me a Bible. To be honest, the Bible wasn't a very useful thing to give me and it didn't interest me in the least. Still, I couldn't refuse it.

My accepting the gift pleased my friend, but if my parents had found out about it they would have been displeased. The reason they would have been upset was because at that time the Catholic priests at home didn't want people reading the Bible. They used to tell adults not to read the Bible and, above all, strongly advised parents not to allow their children to do so. I never understood why this was, except that my country is close to 90 per cent Catholic and the Church—even more so in those days than now—has always been a dominant and, at times, domineering voice in the life of the people. At the present there is no forceful movement to restrain people from reading the Bible. In 1956 it was different, however, and I don't mind saying that I was fearful of being caught with a Bible in my possession. When I got home with my unwanted gift, I hid it in my suitcase. Not once did I give that book a thought. When it came time for me to pack for my return to the United States several months later, I opened up my suitcase—and there was that Bible. As I packed I said to myself, "I'm going to leave this book home." Then I realized that there wasn't any safe hiding place, that if left behind this troublesome book would surely be found by my mother and it would make her very angry. There seemed to be no alternative other than to take that book with me.

After I had been in the States awhile, I discovered that it was nice to have the Bible with me: at least it was written in Spanish and it was something I could read with ease. My English at that time was minimal and, as much as I wanted to learn more of the language by reading newspapers and books, it was a relief to be able to pick up my Bible and read it without having to grope for words and meanings. Other than that, I got no solace from the Bible. Oh, it was pleasant reading and slightly inspirational, but I really didn't understand its message. To me, it seemed like a giant jigsaw puzzle made out of words.

A year later, in 1958, I was playing for Phoenix in the Pacific Coast League and it was while on a trip to Seattle that word arrived for me to come on down and make my big league debut with the Giants. When I checked into the hotel in San Francisco the next day, there was a lengthy cablegram waiting for me. It was from my friend Roque. His wire congratulated me on being called up by the Giants, urged me to read Proverbs 3: 3-7 in the Bible and told me that there was another step upward that I had to take on my own. Roque was hoping that I would understand and that I would become a Christian before playing my first major league game. As far as I knew, I was a Christian; I had gone to church faithfully since childhood.

I spent most of the day thinking about Roque. Some of the words that he had asked me to read kept fluttering around in my mind:

"Trust in the Lord with all thine heart; and lean not unto thine own understanding. In all thy ways acknowledge him, and he shall direct thy paths. Be not wise in thine own eyes: fear the Lord, and depart from evil."

As often as I reread Roque's cable and as often as I looked at Proverbs 3: 3-7, I was moved by merely one thought: this wire must have cost poor, struggling Roque quite a bit of money.

When I awoke the next morning the sun was shining. To myself I thought, "This is going to be a special day." Little did I realize how special that day would be. I could hardly wait to get to Seals Stadium where the Giants were playing in this, their first year on the West Coast. As I put on a Giant uniform for the first time, Al Worthington, a pitcher for the club, came over to my locker. He had spoken to me when I had been at the Giant training camp in Phoenix, Arizona that spring. I was a little leery of him; he had spoken to me about reading my Bible when we were in Arizona and he had even written me a few letters about this matter after I had been farmed out. You don't have to be around Worthington long before realizing that he is a devout man and a man who is as much of a missionary as he is a pitcher. Sure enough, no sooner had he welcomed me to the club than he started talking about the Bible: Had I been reading it? Well, yes. Had I accepted Christ as my personal savior? What?

Within minutes, Worthington explained some of the things in the Bible that had befuddled me. God, he told me, had sent his Son to die on the cross in order to forgive men for their sins and to give to each one who would believe in Him a life everlasting. Portions of Scripture, vaguely remembered and vaguely understood, came to mind and the more Al talked, the more the pieces in this huge jigsaw puzzle fitted together. It hadn't made sense before, mostly because I hadn't wanted it to and because I had only been reading words and had not given them a second thought. My mind was racing, yet attentive. The real meaning of the Bible, of Roque's urgings, of life—they struck me with a clarity and power that stunned me. At some time or other, each of us has given thought to the fact that there is a great mystery to life, that there must be some far deeper reason for life than we can see.

"Do you understand?," Worthington was saying.

"Yes."

"Then now is the time for you to accept Christ into your heart."

"Here?"

"Right here. This is one thing you can't put off."

So, right there, in the middle of the Giant clubhouse, I got down on my knees and asked Christ to cleanse me of my sin and to come into my heart.

Several of the Giants had gathered around and when I arose I saw Pitcher Johnny Antonelli, Infielder Darryl Spencer, Catcher Hobie Landrith and several others staring at me. Then I walked out to the field with Worthington. We played the Cincinnati Reds that day and on the first pitch thrown to me in the big leagues, a fastball by Brooks Lawrence, I singled sharply to left field. My next time up, I again hit the first pitch to left, this time for a double. Getting hits in my first two times up meant a lot to me, but far more meaningful was my acceptance of Christ. Those hits were important for the moment; Christ has been, and will be, important forever.

People often say that the Lord works in strange ways and I marvel at what He did for me, giving me an unwanted Bible, forcing me to take it to the States, getting me to glance at it just enough so that a few words from Al Worthington were sufficient to open my eyes. Looking backward, there was only one regret; had I accepted Christ earlier, it would have made my path so much easier for me during my days as a young player. This is not to say that a Christian life is troublefree. With His help, though, the deep problems that beset me in the beginning would have been less burdensome.

My difficulties began even before I arrived in the United States. There had been no trouble obtaining a passport allowing me to leave the Dominican Republic, but there were complications—what they were, I never did find out—about getting a visa that would permit me to enter the U.S.A. I had been pleased with my first assignment from the Giants, for it seemed poetic-prophetic that they wanted me to go to Melbourne. Alas, the Giants did not mean the Melbourne, Australia that I had once dreamed of, merely Melbourne, Florida, where the club's central training camp was located.

I was supposed to report for spring training early in March, but I had to sit back forlornly and watch the Ides of March as well as the end of March slip by without any visa. Day after day inched by, each an interminable wait. A watched mailman never delivers. Reporting late, I knew, would not enhance my chances of playing with one of the Giants' better farm teams. To take my mind off baseball and to make time pass as swiftly as possible, I attended to all of the incidentals surrounding my eventual trip. Packing my suitcase didn't take much time; there wasn't much to be packed. Had it not been for my trip to the Pan-American Games, I probably wouldn't have had a suitcase and I certainly wouldn't have had much of anything in the way of decent clothing. All members of our Pan-Am team had been given a suitcase and into mine went the dress uniform we wore at the Games—gray slacks, black jacket—and a suit that I had purchased with the $100 spending money each of us had received in Mexico City. Longingly, I gazed at the tiny dot on the map that was Melbourne, Florida and, regretfully, kept notifying the Giants that, no, my visa had not yet arrived. Taking the advice of a friend who had done some travelling, I went to a bank and converted some Dominican money into $48 in American currency.

One day in early April, I decided to go fishing with a friend. The ocean was unusually calm that day; the waves, for once, seemed in no hurry to flail themselves against the shore. If anything, the waves were playing a subdued form of the game of tag that they ceaselessly engage in. Overhead, the sun smiled warmly.

We were in need of bait and decided to use some of the crabs that inhabit that particular area. To get them, we had to go down to the water's edge. First, we peeled off our trousers so they wouldn't get soaked and placed them on a convenient pile of rocks. My $48 in American money was in my trousers. Then the two of us went down to get our crabs, the soft, wet sand squishing playfully between our toes, our feet artfully carving—until the next wave—only momentary proof that we had passed this way. After gathering our bait, we went back to pull on our trousers. As soon as I picked them up I could sense that something was wrong. Sure enough, some enterprising, albeit not honest, soul had taken my $48. No visa. No money. It seemed I was destined not to go to America.

Then, after I had almost given up hope, my visa arrived. On the flight to Miami I began to appreciate how neatly things had fallen into place. A friend of mine had heard that I had lost the $48, so he gave me $10 in American cash. That took care of immediate finances. Sitting next to me on the plane was another friend, a gentleman who had been to the United States numerous times and who had volunteered to point me in the right direction once we arrived in Miami. That took care of immediate travel arrangements. Fortunately, the Giants paid my fare to America. When we got to Miami my friend took me to the Greyhound bus terminal, lined me up on a bus for Melbourne and then waved goodbye. There I stood, alone.

It was a unique sensation to realize that I was in a land I had heard so much about, a land that held out extravagant promises and hopes but which—it suddenly struck me—held not a single known friend. Being on my own like this felt good, though there was already a growing apprehension about the unknowns that lay ahead. It was a relief to know that Alex Pompez, the Giant scout, would be waiting for me at the bus depot in Melbourne, and it was a greater relief to arrive and find that Pompez was actually there. It was April 7, 1956.

For the most part, I felt that the facilities at the Melbourne camp were fine and it was a pleasure to find that there were a number of other Latin ballplayers around. Living quarters were clean, pleasant. And, to make me really feel at home, the sun was fit for broiling. About the only thing that wasn't to my liking was the food: there was no rice, no beans; they kept feeding me steaks; the milk was always so cold. Cooks at Melbourne evidently had no idea in those early days of the Latin breakthrough into baseball that you can't easily change a person's eating habits after 20 years or so. Oh, it can be done, mainly because a hungry player has to eat something. So I nibbled at my steaks, a food that I found to be very rich and one which I had eaten only on rare occasions in the past. And I faithfully drank my cold, cold milk. Back home we always boiled it and drank it warm. Although I did my best, my insides rebelled. Since the age of 16, my weight has been firmly fixed at 194 pounds. That first week in Melbourne, however, was as trying off the field as it was on and I lost quite a bit of weight. Our baseball workouts were much more exacting and much more strenuous than those I had been used to in the Dominican Republic. Running, sliding, bunting, running, hitting, shagging fly balls, running. It sank in quickly: baseball was no longer a game for me; from now on it would be my business.

It hurt me to think that, after all my years of walking and hitch hiking a dozen miles each way to and from high school and college without once ever having been late, I had been more than a month tardy in reporting for the most important date of my life. I was by far the last player to report to Melbourne, a fact that did not go unnoticed.

Originally, the Giants had intended to have me play for their Danville, Virginia affiliate in Class B competition. I worked out just two days with the Danville club and that's all the time it took to realize that I was in no shape to compete with the other players on the roster. Failing with Danville, I was sent by bus to Lake Charles, Louisiana to work out with the Class C team the Giants had in the Evangeline League. Mike McCormick, a national League outfielder of some note throughout the 1940s, was the manager of the Lake Charles team. He, too, took a quick look at me, saw I wasn't ready to play and told me that he couldn't use me, that his team was set and that, furthermore, there was no room for me on the roster. Like the guy who hasn't taken a shower in two weeks, my unpopularity was rapidly becoming unanimous.

Then a rumor started—since I had reported so late and since I was so far behind the other players it might be best to send me back home and have me report to spring training the following year, on time. Alex Pompez heard about it. He stood up for me, defended my position, demanded that I be given a fair chance and insisted that I be placed on the roster. Alex must have been persuasive, for my name was quickly added to the Lake Charles roster.

In my first time at bat as a professional, I got a pinch hit and drove in a run. The next day we were going to play a game against Crowley and I was aware of this. What I wasn't aware of was that this was going to be the start of a five-day road trip. I left Lake Charles completely unprepared—almost penniless and with no change of clothing. For five days I had to borrow money and wear the same clothes. By the end of the trip I couldn't blame the other players if they didn't want to sit next to me on the bus. Still, it was fun being a pro and I was enjoying myself.

One of the oddest things that has ever happened to me in all my years of baseball took place in my second game as a professional. It started innocently, with me speeding back to deep center in a desperate attempt to catch up with a long fly ball. It wasn't even one of those almost-but-not-quite plays: I simply could not outrun the ball and it fell for a hit. The best I could do was come up with the ball on one hop. I turned around to make a quick throw to prevent the runner from getting an inside-the-park homer. As I threw the ball, I saw an umpire out of the corner of my eye and it seemed that he was signalling that I had caught that long drive. It couldn't be. I looked more closely and this time there was no doubt about it; that umpire was convinced that I had made a spectacular catch. By this time, another umpire was giving another signal, indicating that I had accentuated my superlative catch by doubling a runner, who long ago had crossed home plate, off second base. Thus, with a twinge of guilt, I accepted congratulations for not making a catch on a sure triple and turning it into a double play. Even the umpires seemed to be reaching out to give me a helping hand during those days.

CHAPTER 5

"COCOA. ME COCOA. COCOA?"

Just at the time when everything seemed to be going my way, there came some of the most heartsickening news of my life, news that all colored players had been barred from playing in the Evangeline League any longer. Apparently there was a Louisiana law against colored people participating in athletic contests with or against whites. There had been some sort of league meeting to consider this situation and those who did the voting decided that the law had to be upheld and that colored ballplayers were no longer welcome in the Evangeline League.

There is still a notation in the record book which reads: "Baton Rouge forfeited April 28 game to Lake Charles, refusing to play in violation of segregation law because Lake Charles had two Negro players."

Truthfully, I did not understand. I had never heard of any such thing. The racial climate in the U.S. has improved considerably during the past ten years, but then it was almost impossible for me to believe. Back in the Dominican Republic there was never any talk concerning a race problem or racial inequality. Furthermore, my mother is a Caucasian, the daughter of a Spaniard who had migrated to the Dominican Republic. My father is a Negro, the grandson of a slave who had most likely been imported from Africa to work on the farms. There had never appeared to be anything wrong with a man merely because of the color of his skin.

One of the other players got me to understand, more or less, what the situation was like in America—America, the land of the free? What I heard hadn't particularly frightened me, but when word came that the Giants were going to reassign me to the Cocoa Indians in the Florida State League, a Class D menagerie, I almost quit baseball. They say that when you take a Latin out of his native land he soon becomes homesick. Until that time I hadn't been homesick, but the more I thought about family and home, the more serious became my thoughts of returning to the Dominican Republic. About the only thing that kept me from going home was that I wanted to play baseball more than ever. So I got on another bus and rode all the way to Cocoa.

My trip from Melbourne to Lake Charles had not been bad because there were some other Spanish-speaking players on that bus. This trip, however, was a two-and-a-half-day nightmare. Before leaving Lake Charles, I had been given $12 meal money. When I arrived in Cocoa I had spent only 50 cents. Unable to speak any English and unable to read any menus, I was like a little boy lost. Wherever I looked during the frequent bus stops in Mississippi, Alabama, Georgia and Florida there was a sign that I couldn't read but which I was beginning to grasp the awesome power of. It screamed at me from everywhere: COLORED. There were lines at the lunch counters for whites, separate lines for colored people and there is no use in going into details of who got better service and food. This was wrong, I told myself, and I wasn't about to give in even if I was cutting off my source of apple pie to spite my growling stomach.

Aboard the bus I was consigned to the rear. When I noticed that we were in Florida I kept trying to tell the driver that I wanted to get off in Cocoa. I was sure that I was going to miss my stop, so each time we came to a bus stop I would go up to the driver and say, "Cocoa. Me Cocoa. Cocoa?"

"Okay," he would always say.

Near the end of my ride, he had me sit up front, right behind him and when we got to Cocoa he gave me the good news. I appreciated his kindness. It was hard to appreciate the time of day we arrived in Cocoa, though—4:30 in the morning. To myself I thought, "Where do I go now?" Since I had no answer and didn't know how to go about getting one, I did what came naturally—curled up on a bench and went to sleep.

A couple of hours later I awoke, delighted to find the day warm and humid. I thought of how to find two ballplayers—Julio Navarro and Hector Cruz—who played for the Cocoa team and lived somewhere in town. I had met both of them in Melbourne and since they spoke Spanish as well as English, it was imperative that I find them so that I could get a place to live and find out my status as a ballplayer. Not knowing their address didn't help. Not knowing their phone number didn't help. Not being able to converse in English didn't help. Still, as I set forth, my footsteps were lighter than they had been in days. It was probably only because I hadn't eaten and had lost so much weight. All I knew was that somewhere in Cocoa were Navarro and Cruz.

I tried to ask some of the people for help. Nobody paid any attention. I said to one girl, "Navarro? Cruz?"

She looked at me with wide, bewildered eyes. Satisfied that I was not a leftover from last night's bar and sensing that I spoke not a word of her language, she paused. Evidently, she was a bit of a baseball fan, for her reply was, "Ballplayers?"

I nodded my head. What the girl said next I'll never know, but I know she did motion me to get into her car. Within minutes she had driven me to the house where Navarro and Cruz were staying. By now it wasn't much after 8 a.m. and we woke up two very sleepy players. Navarro and Cruz opened a window, hung out and began calling, "Here's the Dominican. Here's the Dominican." That's what they and others had called me in Melbourne.

They hadn't expected me and weren't about to scurry around town to find me a room. "We just played last night in St. Petersburg and got home only a few hours ago," Navarro said. "Why don't you wait around for us, sit on the porch or inside. We'll be up to stay in a few hours."

After having spent several days on a bus, I was not anxious to do any more sitting than was absolutely necessary. What else could I do, though? While I contemplated matters, the girl talked to Navarro and Cruz in English. Julio then told me that the girl knew of a family that would be willing to have me stay as a boarder. Navarro took care of all the translating, got me to agree to look at the place the girl had spoken of and got her to consent to drive me over there.

I've had my share of shocks and that morning I got one that still lingers. When we got to the house the girl had in mind, I was jolted, for there, at about 9 a.m., was a party going on, a real swingin', hard drinking, raucous, whoop-it-up party.

"I don't think this is the best place for me to stay," I thought. For the moment, however, there was little I could do about the situation. Between hunger and weariness I was immobilized. When the lady of the house had showed me to a room, I plopped into bed with my shoes and clothes on—I was afraid to take anything off—and went to sleep. The next thing I knew, it was 4 in the afternoon.

The woman—all I can recall is that her name was Blanche—motioned for me to come downstairs for dinner. It was a meal that I can still envision: corn bread, sweet potatoes, fried chicken and—hallelujah—rice. Blanche and her husband didn't speak Spanish, but this didn't keep them from talking to me. By using some of the standards of universal sign language—nodding or shaking my head, pointing to something, smiling, shrugging my shoulders, rubbing my stomach— I managed to more or less (mostly less, I suppose) hold my own during this mealtime chitchat. From time to time I glanced outside, where several leftovers from the party were still dancing. As hospitable as Blanche and her husband were and as good as the food tasted, I was already forming plans to move elsewhere, to a quieter place.

Baseball had almost completely slipped my mind until Navarro and Cruz stopped at the house to pick me up on their way to the ball park. They didn't exactly pick me up. What it amounted to was that they asked me to join them in walking the rest of the way to the stadium, which was about a half-mile away. They asked me how I liked the place where I was staying. My reply was that the abundance of hospitality, as greatly appreciated as it was, could not compensate for the lack of sobriety.

"Sleep there tonight," Navarro advised me, "and tomorrow we'll try to find another place for you."

When I stepped into the clubhouse at the park, I could see that here were worse accommodations than the ones I had just been complaining about. This place did not deserve to be called a clubhouse. It was little more than a cave chiseled out of the side of a hill—a dank, narrow corridor in which there was hardly room to suit up. Woe be unto the player who was a slow dresser; he would be set upon by hordes of mosquitoes and reduced to a mass of welts.

Standing in the dugout and looking out at the playing field that I earnestly hoped would become my baseball home was a semi-pleasant experience. For one thing, it was discouraging to realize that this was the third team I had been with in less than one month during my steady decline from Class B to Class C to Class D. It was much more soothing to contemplate what Buddy Kerr, the manager of this Cocoa team, had said to me in the clubhouse-cave. Kerr had no more than met me and given me a warm handshake than he told me that I was going to be his regular center fielder. That's the kind of news I had been longing to hear. Nevertheless, I felt dragged-out, as though the hearty meal and the long nap had been too much for my weary body to take all at once.

After the game I felt better than I had all day. I had picked up my first hit as a member of the Cocoa Indians, something that does wonders for making a hitter feel like he belongs. The scene in the clubhouse-cave that night was reminiscent of a madcap cartoon as players leaped, jiggled from one foot to another, snapped towels and fought for elbow room—all in an effort to get dressed before the mosquitoes did irreparable damage. A couple of my new teammates were telling me that I was lucky to be so big because one of the players who was no longer with the club hadn't lost his job because of poor hitting, he'd simply been carried off by a swarm of mosquitoes. This was hardly the sort of story that even a raw recruit like me was about to fall for, but after a batch of those tiny dive bombers had assaulted me for the first time I was willing to believe anything.

That night when I got to the house where I was staying I was pleasantly surprised to find that quiet rather than merry-making prevailed. The next day Navarro told me that Blanche had called and asked him to explain to me that she and her husband were going to New York City for two months and that during their absence I could have the house to myself. With Blanche's permission, I had Jim Miller, the second baseman on the team, move in with me and for the next two months we lived in quiet luxury. Even after Blanche and her husband returned, the house remained relatively peaceful. There was never another party of any consequence and, as far as I could figure out, the one I had stumbled into had apparently been a going-away affair.

Minor league finances being what they are, our team rarely stayed out of town. The only town we occasionally holed up in (I use the expression advisedly) was Gainesville. There the team always split into two groups, the whites going to one hotel, the colored to another. I have no idea what sort of hotel the whites stayed in. All I know is that the one we were sent to was in the colored section of town and that the floors in our second-story rooms were so rickety that we were afraid to walk on them for fear they would collapse.

With hotels such as this to choose from, it was best that we didn't stay overnight too often, even if it did mean piling into the club's two station wagons and not getting back to Cocoa until almost dawn sometimes. These were the sort of trips that have made Class D baseball travel so infamous. By the time we had crammed 16 players, one manager and assorted equipment bags into them, the rideability of these cars had been reduced to that of Conestoga Wagons. Unlike the Conestogas, however, our station wagons had flat tires. Lots of them.

If you want to find out about a state, one of the best ways to accomplish this, I learned, is to have flat tires at any hour of the day or night and at any place from a busy intersection to the most desolate hinterlands. This allows ample time to roam around, study the countryside, the birds, traffic, weather and, above all, the oranges. We had flats almost daily and while they were being repaired we would invariably scout through local orchards and yards for oranges, carrying them back by the armload and dumping them wherever we could find any room in the station wagons. One day we overdid it, filling the station wagon so full of oranges that they covered up the back window.

We were young and eager players and the bounce and zest, the enthusiasm and humor of youth made even the worst trips endurable. One of the few things that bothered me to any extent was the language barrier. About the first thing I had done after signing to play ball in the United States was to invest around $75 in a Hollywood course that was going to teach me how to speak, read and write English almost instantly. When I got to the United States I found that English is English but that what Americans speak is American. Living in the drawl-heavy South did not help. Nowhere on the records or in the textbooks that had been sent to me from Hollywood was there anything similar to, "Y'all come'n back tumarrah, heah?"

It was not so difficult getting used to American food, southern style. After the first few times around, I began to enjoy hush puppies, fried catfish and grits. I ate all my meals at a restaurant in Cocoa with Navarro, Cruz and Miller.

The other players were well aware that, since I had been signed to a Class B contract originally and had to be paid accordingly, I was earning more money than the rest of the players, $275 a month to be exact. This was something they never let me forget. Navarro, Cruz and Miller continually made references to my higher income and urged me to share my wealth by treating them to postgame snacks. I was more than glad to do this now and then, though it must be admitted that my ability to do so stemmed not so much from the few extra dollars that I was earning as it did from the generosiy of local fans.

Those fans in Cocoa had a custom that put the frosting on the cake, or at least made it possible for me to buy some cake in the first place. When a Cocoa player came through with a spectacular performance, the hometown rooters often would pass the hat through the stands and turn over the proceeds to the reigning hero. One night I came to bat with two men on base in the bottom of the ninth inning of a game in which West Palm Beach had us beaten 2-0. I hit a home run over the left field fence for a 3-2 victory, one of my first and most memorable thrills as a professional. What made it even more memorable was that the fans passed the hat and presented me with $89.

After weeks of being shunted from one club to another and feeling unwanted, it was gratifying to know that I had now found a home. That night I could hardly wait to treat Navarro, Cruz and Miller to hamburgers and as much cake, frosting and all, as they could devour. Thereafter, Navarro kept saying to me, "Come on, hit a home run for us tonight. We're short on money and we're hungry." We ate well that season.

Navarro, had he wanted to, could have passed as a white man. He counseled me daily, telling me about things I could and could not do, places I could and could not go because my skin was tan, something that supposedly made me inferior to people whose skin was white. Patiently, Navarro kept brain-washing me, telling me about how Jackie Robinson and others had survived and succeeded, telling me that there wasn't anything that I could do about the race situation and that I should learn to live with it.

"Patience, Felipe. You must have patience." This was Julio talking. It wasn't easy.

Without Buddy Kerr, the former Giant second baseman for a manager it would have been impossible. He kept me in baseball. I could sense that Kerr was somewhat embarrassed about what had been going on. He went out of his way to be kind and helpful to me. When opposing pitchers would throw at me, Buddy would come out on the field ready to defend me and, in fact, did defend me, both verbally and with threatening gestures that made it clear to everyone that he was on my side in more ways than one. He used to take me aside and encourage me. Buddy would tell me that I was a good prospect and that if I didn't let the race situation bother me I would make it to the majors. He told me of others who had persevered and made it. I can still hear him saying, "Those guys weren't any better than you and they made it. All you have to do is to follow their example and keep trying harder."

His words meant a lot to me, but they couldn't knock down the barriers. One night Buddy found out just how deeply prejudiced man can be. After night games at home, players from our club used to go to a restaurant for something to eat. White players were allowed to eat in the dining room, colored players in a yard out back. One night, we pulled into the parking lot next to the restaurant and a waitress came out and told the colored players—Jim Miller of Miami and Chuck Howard of Baltimore were with me—that she would serve us right there. We thanked her, but before she could even take our orders along came the proprietor.

"Don't you know where their place is?" he yelled at the girl.

Miller and Howard got out of the station wagon and ran away into the night. I didn't understand much English yet and wasn't sure of what was going on. The more the owner ranted and raved, though, the more certain I was that he took exception to my tan skin. It revolted me and when the owner left I just sat in the station wagon, waiting for my teammates so that I could go back to my room. My appetite was gone; just thinking about racial intolerance made me sick to my stomach.

Within minutes, a police car pulled into the parking lot. Two policemen got out and walked toward me. They said something to me which made no sense. Then I understood one of them telling me to open the door and that if I didn't he was going to pull me out of the station wagon. My temper was volcanic but my mind was set:

I wasn't going to get out, no matter what. Too often had I been humiliated. Too often had I been made to feel ashamed of the color of my skin. A fleeting thought crossed my mind and I vowed that, if need be, I was willing to die right there rather than make any further concessions. When one of the policemen reached for my arm, I rattled off some strong Spanish words to him. He backed away.

By this time, some of my teammates saw what was going on and they got Kerr to come on the double. One policeman told Kerr that I was a rebel, that I wasn't supposed to be in the parking lot and that the owner had argued with me and had then called for police help. Kerr looked at me with eyes as sad as those of a sick puppy dog. He asked me to leave. Buddy said that there was nothing he could do under the circumstances. I told him I wouldn't leave. Finally, Buddy got in and drove the station wagon out of the lot and waited across the street for the other players. When I got back to my room that night I knew a loneliness and despair that made me ache all over.

There were other tribulations that first season. Pitchers—even some from my own team—used me for target practice; opposing pitchers would send me sprawling in the dirt during games and teammates would do the same in batting practice. Once I overheard several of my teammates instructing pitchers on another team what pitches I had been hitting well and what ones had been giving me trouble. My first inclination was to repay these traitorous teammates by banging their heads together. Fortunately, this thought was soon replaced by more rational ones. I realized that the ones who were betraying me were among the youngest members of our team—they were teenagers, whereas I was an elderly 20—and that this faithlessness was typical of their teenage behavior.

As my temper cooled, my hostile attitude was replaced by a conviction that no pitcher, no matter how well informed he might be about my supposed weaknesses at the plate, was going to get me out. This case of superconfidence stemmed largely from the hitting streak I had currently been on, a spree during which I had 15 hits in 19 trips to the plate. There remains a vivid memory that this splurge had left me with a batting average of .433 and, evidently, a newfound assurance in my abilities. As it was, I had underestimated both the effectiveness of even a Class D grapevine, which spread the glad news about the chinks in my armor, and the Class D pitchers, who made efficient use of the tips they had been given. My batting average dropped like a marble coming down from Pike's Peak, skidding more than 50 points before the season came to a close. There wasn't any local newspaper in Cocoa and, because of that and because I couldn't read the papers that *were* available, it was hard for me to keep up with what was going on throughout the league. All I knew was that our club, which had won the first half of the pennant race by half a game, was well in front in the second half and that I was leading the league in hitting by a large margin. Or so I thought.

We were in a restaurant in the Negro section of Daytona Beach before a game there one day when I was glancing through a newspaper to see if there was anything that I could decipher. I got a real jolt. With help from Navarro, I found out that Don Dillard of Daytona Beach had taken the batting lead away from me. I knew that he had gone 5 for 5 the night before against us in Cocoa, but had assumed that I was still well ahead of him. The story in the paper said that Dillard had come from far behind to overtake me and that he had no plans to relinquish the lead. I actually felt a little frightened when I realized that I had been living in such ignorance. Throughout the day I could feel myself getting keyed up for the game. In that game I went 5 for 6, Dillard 1 for 4 and from then on I held on to the batting lead. It was a good thing that I had that big day against Daytona Beach, for I wound up beating out Dillard by just five points—.380 to .375. I also led the league in stolen bases with 48, was third in runs scored with 111, three behind the leader, who played in 17 more games than I did. In home runs I wound up third with a total of 21, just one behind the co-leaders in that department.

Navarro led the league with a record of 24 wins and 8 losses and was also first with an earned run average of 2.16. Very few of the players in that league made it all the way to the majors. Cookie Rojas, a real good handyman for the Philadelphia Phillies in recent years, hit .275 for West Palm Beach that season. And Dave Bristol, who became the manager of the Cincinnati Reds midway through the 1966 season, played third base and batted .274 for West Palm Beach in 1956.

It had been a gratifying season for me in many ways. After it was all over, I received a check for $200 from the Giants. That constituted my bonus from the Giants, a sum they had promised to pay me only if I made whatever team they ultimately assigned me to during my first year of professional ball. The $200 was quickly used to help pay off some of the family debts. Another little something that I was thankful for was that I had at last wound up in a league where I hadn't had to worry about the tormentor who had deprived me of those two batting championships in the Dominican Republic.

CHAPTER 6

MARIA AND THE MAJORS

Being back home in Haina after my first season in the States was even more enjoyable than I had imagined it would be. Seeing my family and friends again was part of it. Getting back to boiled plantain and home-cooked rice was more of it. Then, too, I found that my .380 batting average had given me new stature. Beyond this was even more—being able to speak Spanish all the time, being able to swim and fish whenever I pleased and, above all, having the chance to see Maria. I had known Maria Beltre for a number of years, but our friendship was little more than that, just a friendship, a nod of hello, a few words here and there. During the five months that I was home between seasons, however, I saw a lot of Maria, and our friendship became much deeper, much richer.

I remember one night a few years earlier when I tried very hard to impress her and came out second best to a dog. It all took place at a show where there were some trained dogs who were supposed to be more intelligent than human beings. The man who was handling the dogs said that he was going to prove his point and wanted to know if there were any humans who thought they might be smarter than his animals. Here, I thought, was my chance to dazzle Maria. Confident that there was no way that a dog could show me up, I volunteered.

As I stood in front of Maria and the rest of the audience, the dog handler explained that he would call out a number from 1 to 10. My unenviable job, the handler went on to say, was to try to beat the dog in finding the card with the designated number from a batch of cards spread on the floor. I still did not feel the slightest bit of apprehension. After all, I had always had good marks in school and, as a matter of fact, had done very well while in college. Beating a dog in a contest of wits wouldn't be an awful lot to boast about, but for some reason I thought that it would be a little something that would make Maria proud of me. No sooner had the handler called out the number—7 I think it was—than I was on the search for the right card. Here was No. 6, there was No. 3 and right over there was, oops.

What was that dog doing? Oh no, he had found No. 7. The crowd laughed and laughed, and then laughed some more. Through it all, the dog pranced around, a proud, happy winner. What would Maria think? Someday when I was older I would run for dog catcher, maybe, and then I would get even with that mutt.

It was a humiliation that did not linger, for, after all, it was pretty funny to be outsmarted by a dog. Soon I was able to laugh about the incident—and Maria laughed with me. Maria and I spent a lot of time together during the winter of 1956-57, though our dates were hardly the kind that would make the gossip columns. Our courtship consisted mainly of my going to her home. That was it, I would go to her home and we would sit and talk and look at each other. When I really felt reckless, I would hold Maria's hand. It wasn't really all that mild, because I soon found that I was in love with Maria and the sparkle in Maria's eyes told me that maybe she could love me in return—even if I wasn't as smart as a dog.

I had known Maria since she was about six years old. She had been born in the southern part of the country and when she was two or three years old her family had moved to Haina. She was several years younger than I was, which meant that we saw very little of each other throughout our school days. I had taken an early, if distant, liking to Maria and felt that it was a pretty good sign that it had been my father who had built her family's home in Haina.

Before that winter was over Maria and I were talking about marriage. When a couple starts this sort of conversation in the Dominican Republic, the proper thing to do is to go to the parents for permission to become engaged. Thus it was that I went to my father and explained matters. My father then spoke to Maria's dad and, since both fathers were in agreement that our marriage would be a good thing, we obtained their consent and were formally engaged.

There was further good news that winter in the form of a letter from the Giants notifying me that they were assigning me to their Class AAA Minneapolis farm team in the American Association for the 1957 season. When I took off for spring training a few weeks after receiving that letter, however, I felt even emptier than the year before. This time I was leaving behind the girl I loved, as well as my family.

In 1957 the Giants had their central spring training camp for their minor league clubs in Sanford, Florida. After having played almost the entire season in Florida the year before, I was beginning to feel that the state was my second home. I didn't really appreciate Florida, however, until after I left it and arrived in Minneapolis and felt the first bite of the cold midwestern wind. We played a preseason exhibition game in Minneapolis against the Braves, formerly of Boston, later of Atlanta, but at that moment of Milwaukee. That was the day I saw my first snow. It had snowed the night before and the ground crew had shoveled the snow into piles around the fringe of the field. During the game, one of the Braves hit a ball into one of those mounds that dotted the rim of the outfield. I had to reach into that mound to retrieve the ball and it was at that moment that I touched snow for the first time. I didn't like the sensation at all. Milwaukee led 3-0 going ino the last of the ninth inning, but Carlos Paula hit a three-run homer for us, making a lot of enemies in the process as he forced us all to trudge back out into the cold. None of us felt too sad when Wes Covington gave the Braves a 4-3 win when he homered in the 10th inning.

That brief encounter with snow was about the only thing that I didn't enjoy about my 1957 spring training period. With a springtime batting average of .387, I had little trouble making the Minneapolis team. Egged on by grandiose thoughts of my .380 batting average of the year before and of my .387 that spring, I began to think that maybe I could hit in the .380s no matter what league I was sent to. Hah!

As soon as the American Association season got underway, opposing pitchers did an excellent job of knocking such fanciful notions from my mind. The cold weather didn't help any, either. For the first time in my life I experienced the unpleasant sensation of being cold for an extended period. It made me feel ill at ease, unnatural, further away from home than ever. More than anything else, I suppose that my sudden inability to hit the ball was simply because I was not yet ready for AAA competition. It was merciful that after one month I was shipped to the Springfield, Massachusetts club in the Class A Eastern League. At the time of my departure from Minneapolis, I had been in 24 games, had not hit any home runs and my batting average had come to an inglorious rest at .211.

When I got to Springfield I was happy to find that Julio Navarro, my friend from Cocoa, was also on the team. We had a pleasant reunion and then I began to do some serious thinking. No one likes to be demoted, but I felt that it would be good for me to get away from Minneapolis, my .211 average and the cold. The first two were easy to escape. Springfield, though, turned out to be colder than Minneapolis. Catching line drives on those frigid nights was like trying to latch on to flying ice cubes. I could almost feel the bones crack and was fearful of taking my glove off to look, because I was certain my fingers would drop off like so many slivers of broken glass.

Although it was cold in Springfield, I knew that this could never be used as an excuse for not performing well. For the first time in my career I began to think that I had a legitimate chance to be a big-leaguer some day. Reflecting upon my good year with Cocoa and my brief stay with Minneapolis, I could see that if I had another good season or two I might be called up by the Giants. I made up my mind to hustle more than ever before so that whatever talents I had would not be wasted.

In my spare time I wrote a flurry of letters to Maria. And I also began reading the unwanted Bible that had been kept hidden in my suitcase throughout the winter.

To say that the Bible suddenly became very dear to me and that I had a voracious appetite for reading it would be a lie. I read it because it was there and because it was written in Spanish and it was easy to read. There was much of the Bible that I did not understand and I made no concerted effort to try to figure things out.

Most of my energies were concentrated on the baseball field. After my poor record with Minneapolis, I felt that I had to prove myself all over again. With a renewed dedication, I tried harder than ever. In my first game for Springfield I had to bat against Ed Dick of Binghamton, who wound up as the winningest pitcher in the Eastern League with an 18-9 record. I had a couple of hits that night and, running at top speed in center field, made a good catch of a long drive hit by Fred Carpenter of Binghamton.

On one of my first road trips I made my annual mistake of forgetting to bring along my equipment. It was decided that I should wear the uniform, spikes and glove belonging to Al Vincent, a left-handed pitcher on our club. I felt very bad about this because it meant that, since he did not have a uniform now, he could not pitch in a single game on our road trip. I felt guilty and thought that the only way I could redeem myself was by hitting the ball hard. Luckily, I did just that. During a doubleheader on that trip I had seven consecutive hits, drove in seven runs and stole four bases. I was utilizing my speed better than ever—I doubt that my father could have caught me during those days—and in my first 20 games with Springfield had 15 stolen bases.

Everything seemed to be going right. My salary was $600 a month and out of that I took just enough to pay for my room, meals and a few incidentals. All the rest of the money was sent home to my parents. Even the travelling conditions were worth writing home about. Our team had to make some long trips, but we went by bus and it was possible to stretch out and take a nap. In a way, I missed the oranges and the warmth and the flat tires that were so much a part of Class D ball with Cocoa, but when I would check into a nice clean hotel in Reading or Allentown, Pennsylvania and find that there was no worry about walking across the floor, I was grateful.

What's more, I was now playing in the northern part of the country and there were no more signs bearing the vicious word COLORED. I could eat in any restaurant I wanted to, could sit in any seat on any bus and not have to worry about a thing. My manager once again was Mike McCormick, the man I had first played under at Lake Charles. I had taken a genuine liking to McCormick during my brief stay in Lake Charles, even though he must take credit for having irrevocably botched up the pronounciation of my name. No sooner had I reported to the Lake Charles team than McCormick had started calling me Phil Alou. Phil didn't stick, but Alou certainly did. Although I don't mind what has been done to my name, I would like to point out a few facts about my name and how our family feels it should be pronounced.

My correct name is Felipe Rojas Alou. In Latin countries the mother's maiden name is tacked on to the names of all her children and comes *after* the husband's name. Thus, Rojas is my father's name, Alou my mother's maiden name. I think that this arrangement is both a quaint custom which enables a woman to retain *her* family name and a convenient way of tracing lineage. In many other parts of the world people don't pay as close attention to ancestry as we do. This is true in America and after just a few weeks in the country I was divested of my family name of Rojas. McCormick was not trying to be nasty when he gave me a new name. He just said that he thought Alou was easier to remember and to pronounce than Rojas.

I didn't argue, mainly because I *couldn't* argue. It was hard getting used to Alou instead of Rojas at first, but the reason for that was that the people were mispronouncing the name. They were pronouncing it A'-lou. It should be pronounced A-loo'. My great-grandfather on my mother's side was a Frenchman and undoubtedly was called A-lou. Our family feels that despite the French nature of the name it should be given a Spanish pronunciation now that we live in a land that does not use French as its basic language. When all three Alou brothers are hitting well, people in the Dominican Republic say that "the telephone is working," which is a play on the word used when they answer the telephone—"Aloo." Actually, when I am at home people always refer to me as Felipe Rojas Alou. That is the way they refer to me on radio, in the newspapers and in conversation, and that is the way my mail is addressed. In America my paychecks have always been made out to Felipe R. Alou. I have never had any trouble cashing any of them, so I really can't complain too much.

Being on the same team with Julio again was nice. Jose Pagan, a

Puerto Rican who was to become very dear to me in the years that followed, was also on our team and the three of us spent many hours together. Cold as it was, I soon took a liking to Springfield and still regard it as one of the finest cities I have ever known. Our team was not a good one, though, and we wound up 29½ games out of first place. Outside of that, everything was going so well that it seemed unreal.

Reality has a way of creeping up on you when you least expect it, though, and that's precisely what happened to me. My awakening came when, goaded on by my all-out determination to try my hardest, I attempted to score all the way from first base on a single. I scored all right, but somehow tripped over home plate and fell flat on my face. In the process, I severely injured a muscle in my right leg. An injury in the minor leagues often proves to be more disastrous than in the majors because proper medical attention is so much harder to come by. Minor league trainers are usually not much help. They simply are not as well trained, as well equipped or as dedicated as their major league counterparts. Thus it was that neither I nor the club was made aware of the full extent of my injury.

Three days after being hurt, I was given permission by the trainer to resume playing. Anxious to do something beside sit on the bench, I was happy to get back in the lineup, even though my leg still throbbed. It was a costly mistake. I reinjured my leg in the first game I played and was unable to perform well for the remainder of the season. At the time I had originally injured my leg my batting average was .389. My leg did not respond to what little treatment I could get and for the rest of the year I was reduced to being a pinch hitter and bit-part player. With my speed and timing impaired, my batting average plummeted to .306 by the end of the season. What had looked like a good year had wound up as pretty much of a washout.

That injury to my leg had far-reaching consequences. Even now the muscle bulges hard and rocklike, a sign that it never healed properly. Furthermore, I am convinced that the injury was at least partly responsible for a much more serious leg ailment that necessitated an operation and nearly ended my career in 1964.

Statistics give some indication of how much my speed has been impaired. Over a period of 139 games—119 with Cocoa and my first 20 with Springfield—I had 63 stolen bases, an average of almost one every other game. Then came the injury to my leg. In 1,278 games in the majors and minors since that time, I have stolen only 82 bases, or about one each 16 games. To blame this decline in base stealing entirely on an old injury, however, would neither be fair nor correct. As so often is the case, statistics do not tell the full story. In this instance there is another important reason why my base stealing has declined so sharply. Starting with the Phoenix club I played for at the beginning of the 1958 season and going right through the present, I have been associated with teams that have been chock full of sluggers. In Phoenix I was in the same lineup with such long-ball hitters as Willie McCovey, Leon Wagner and Willie Kirkland. Later, with the San Francisco Giants, there were Willie Mays, Orlando Cepeda and, once again, McCovey, among a cast of thousands. With the Braves, I have been surrounded by such home run hitters as Hank Aaron, Eddie Mathews, Joe Torre, Rico Carty, Mack Jones and Denis Menke.

In eight of the nine years that I have spent in the National League, I have played for clubs that have been no worse than second in home runs. During the past five seasons I have played for clubs that have averaged 193 home runs and have led the league in that department four times. The gist of all this is that teams such as this don't rely much on stealing bases to produce runs. They sit back and wait for the fence-clearing drives that bring super-quick runs.

As exciting as the home run may be to the fan and the hitter—yes, we still get that electric sensation down the middle of the back when we hit one out—it will never be the answer to having a winning baseball team. Despite all the home runs that have been hit by the teams I have been on, only one of those clubs has been a pennant winner. I am glad that home run hitting is not the overriding factor in deciding pennants, glad in the sense that baseball is a more complete game than that. Baseball is a game of both offense and defense and, perhaps as important as any other one item, the ever-present intangibles. Into this last category fall such hard-to-explain factors as attitude, desire and the ability to capitalize on the unexpected and illogical situations.

During the weeks that I hobbled around the Eastern League on my bad leg, I experienced periods of anxiety. As the pain in my leg persisted and as my batting average fell lower and lower, I could feel an ebb in my attitude and desire. When McCormick was fired during the middle of the season I felt doubly bad: not only had I lost a good friend, but I felt responsible for his having been cut loose. If I hadn't been so anxious to try to play, all might have worked out well. As it was, I was eager to resume play when the trainer gave his approval. I was aware that the Giants were getting reports concerning my on-field performances and I wanted them to be favorable. They were not terribly upset when they found out I had been injured the first time, for the report evidently indicated nothing serious. When the Giants inquired about me a few weeks later and learned that I had been hurt again, there were some angry people in the San Francisco front office. A few days later McCormick was gone.

There were times when I would read my Bible, feeling that there might be help to be found there. It had been a source of comfort and inspiration to others, I had heard, but to me it remained little more than pleasant reading. For the first time, though, I began to ponder some of the things I had read and there seemed to be portions that made sense to me. No longer was the Bible just a collection of beautifully told stories and moral reminders. I began to realize that there was more to Christ than anyone had ever told me and yet I could not bring myself to fully contemplate just what He meant and stood for. In the recesses of my mind there was a brake that always seemed to be applied precisely at the moment when I was nearing a deeper understanding of what Christ meant when he said, "Come unto me, all ye that labour and are heavy laden, and I will give you rest" (Matthew 11: 28, KJV). Like so many other people, I suppose that I could sense that my cares really could be cast away and that there was an assurance of rest and peace to be had. And like so many others, I suppose that I was, in some strange way, enjoying my unrest and was afraid to find out too much about this Jesus of the Bible. There is a certain amount of satisfaction in self-pity and I feel that it is because of this that so many of us tend to apply the brakes and park in spiritual oblivion.

When I arrived in the Dominican Republic after my disappointing 1957 season, I felt a release from the frustrations of the past months. The medicinal benefits of home, family and loved ones often far exceed those administered under clinical care. Bolstering my spirits even further that winter was some mail that I received from San Francisco. I was notified that I had been promoted to the Giants' No. 1 farm club in Phoenix and that my salary had been raised to $750 a month. On top of that came instructions telling me to join the Giants themselves for spring training at their major league base in Phoenix. I looked forward to meeting the Giant players, but my enthusiasm was tempered by the realization that I had been invited so that club officials could give me a quick look and not because I was to get a real chance to make the roster. Nonetheless, it was an encouraging winter and by the time I reported to Phoenix in 1958 my morale was quite a bit higher than it had been when I had left Springfield.

My suspicion that I wouldn't be given an opportunity to make the Giant team couldn't have been more accurate. Not once did I start any of the exhibition games played by the Giants. My only job was to take over for Willie Mays in center field when he was removed along about the seventh inning of many of the games. The only chance I had to get in some extended competition was during intrasquad games at the very outset of spring training. Even if I do say so myself, I must admit that I created quite an impression on Giant Manager Bill Rigney in one of those contests, so much so that he called me aside and had a few confidential words to say to me. I was thankful that his words were confidential, because they went something like, "How could you make a stupid play like that?"

It seems that Rigney was perturbed because I had made a throw from center field to the wrong base, thereby allowing a runner to move up an extra base. I felt that Rigney's question deserved an answer. Then I tried to figure out how I was going to explain that I had thrown the ball to the wrong base because everybody on both sides was a Giant and that they all wore the same uniforms, a condition that made it impossible for me to tell who was doing what. I had absolutely no difficulty thinking of how to clarify the whole mess for Rigney in 50 well-chosen words. Unfortunately, the words would have been in Spanish. In what was probably one of the wiser decisions of my career, I remained silent. I was glad not to make the Giant varsity, figuring that if I could stay away from Rigney for a while he might forget all about me. Little did I realize how soon I would be seeing him again.

The Phoenix team that I played for in the Pacific Coast League that year was crammed with sluggers. On this club there was no such thing as the coach or manager giving you a steal sign. All they signaled for was the home run. When I first got to Phoenix, I roomed with a Panamanian player named Bobby Prescott. We lived in such a small place that I later accepted an invitation from a wealthy Negro woman named Mrs. Phillips, the owner of the apartment, to move in with her family. Willie McCovey accepted a similar invitation and we each wound up with a nice clean room to ourselves in her home.

Unfortunately, the transportation to the ball park hardly matched the quality of our rooms. McCovey drove me to the park each day in a pile of junk that had four wheels, a license plate and the ability to bluff its way through traffic on the pretense that it was a car. I still say that it was that contraption that led to my being called up so quickly by the Giants. That car had a terminal radiator disorder. The only way to keep the buggy going from one breath to another was to keep a sharp eye out for gas stations so that I could run inside, get a can of water, run back to the car and fill up the sievelike radiator. By the time I put the radiator cap on, closed the hood and got back in the car it was time to start looking for another gas station. All this extra exercise put me in A-1 condition, which helped me to hit better, which prompted the Giants to bring me to San Francisco in June.

My two months with Phoenix under Manager Red Davis were

among the best I have ever put in as a player. Davis used me as a leadoff batter, something that I was not accustomed to. I got used to this quickly and in 55 games wound up hitting 16 doubles and 13 homers, driving in 42 runs and batting .319.

Even though I had been in the minor leagues for less than two and a half years when word came for me to report to San Francisco, I felt confident. Getting those two hits in my first game helped. Three days after I had become a Giant, I hit my first home run in the majors off Vernon Law of the Pittsburgh Pirates. I got an even greater sense of satisfaction out of what I did in a game a little more than a week after being brought up. This was the final game of our home stand and Al Worthington, who had been doing almost nothing except relief pitching all season, was being given his first start in nearly two months. I knew the game meant a lot to Al. That's why I was so pleased when I got a single, double and triple, drove in one run and scored two others as he beat the Phillies 3-1.

During those early days in the National League I had little trouble hitting any of the pitchers. In our next game, which was in Pittsburgh, I homered over the scoreboard in left field in my first at bat, giving me a single, double, triple and home run in my past four times up. My next time up, I hit a line drive to right field. It was a base hit all the way—until the Pirate right fielder came flying out of nowhere to make a diving catch. Right at that moment I found out who Roberto Clemente was. That was the first of many outs I was to make in the next few weeks. It didn't take major league pitchers long to discover that I had a knack of waiting on pitches and that I could hit curveballs better than fastballs. Soon I was removed from the regular lineup and allowed to play only against left-handed pitchers.

When my batting average started to tumble, a number of people began saying and writing that my trouble was that I was shy and homesick. It is true that I was shy, for this is a trait that lingers with me to some extent even now. There were no feelings of homesickness, however, and I would like to have that popular misconception done away with. On the same team with me were a couple of righthanded Latin pitchers, Ruben Gomez, a Puerto Rican, and Ramon Monzant, a Venezuelan. Also on the club was Orlando Cepeda, the big first baseman from Puerto Rico. We had been teammates briefly in Minneapolis the year before, but whereas I had been sent to Springfield, Cepeda stayed on and had a fine season (25 home runs, 108 runs batted in and a .309 batting average). Orlando became the regular first baseman for the Giants in 1958. He also became my closest friend, as well as my roommate.

There was one night in Philadelphia when the two of us were

seized simultaneously by a state of bankruptcy and by boundless appetites. This was one of those paydays—ballplayers are paid on the 1st and 15th of each month during the season—when our checks did not come through on time, something that happens every once in a while when on the road. When you are broke there isn't much you can do. We counted our money and it came to 16 cents. Orlando, I think, had nine cents. He asked for my pennies and I gave them to him. Then he went into a little restaurant and bought a cup of soup. I may have been naive enough to have given away what little money I had, but there wasn't a touch of homesickness anywhere. Just listening to Orlando chatter in Spanish was enough to make me feel at home.

Although Cepeda almost duplicated the year he had had in Minneapolis by getting 25 home runs, 96 runs batted in and hitting .312, I was having more and more problems hitting the ball. Manager Bill Rigney had every right to get as perturbed with me as he had when I had thrown the ball to the wrong base during spring training. Soon I couldn't even get any hits against lefthanded pitchers and Rigney removed me from the lineup altogether. I waved goodbye to my batting average, which wound up at .253, and began counting the days until I could head for home, Haina and Maria.

CHAPTER 7

THE OPEN BOOK

Knowing that he would be interested in what had happened, I had written a letter to Roque Martinez shortly after I had accepted Christ, telling him how grateful I was for his cable and for his faithfulness to me. Roque told other people back home about what I had written him and when I returned to the Dominican Republic that fall dozens of them asked why I had made such a decision. While at home, I joined a local church of the Plymouth Brethren denomination. This I did mainly because Roque was a member of this church, but I had given the matter considerable thought earlier and had decided to leave the Catholic Church.

Although I knew exactly why I had made such a decision, it was and still is hard to explain to my people. This is primarily because there is a no more delicate topic to discuss than religion and it is for this reason that I wish to clarify my stand at this time. To begin with, many people felt that my leaving the Catholic Church signified a hatred for Catholicism and for Catholics. This is not true. How could I harbor any such hatred or dislike when every adult member of my family except my wife is Catholic? I love these people and respect their religious convictions, even if I don't agree with them. I don't think they dislike me for my Christian stand any more than I dislike them because they are Catholic. They disagree with me, and I will not deny this, but I believe that they recognize the sincerity of my decision, just as I respect their sincerity. In fact, my two oldest children—Maria and Felipe—attend a Catholic school in Santo Domingo. I have sent them to this school because I believe it offers the best education, the best discipline and the most safety that can be had in Santo Domingo.

One of the first things I became aware of after I had made my decision in the Giant clubhouse was that, although I had attended services in Catholic churches in the Dominican Republic for years, I had heard little about Jesus Christ. I began to wonder about this, to ask myself how there could be Christianity without Christ.

I recall that often during my thoughts there came back the memory of a holy day when a statue of Mary, the mother of Jesus, was taken from the Catholic church in Haina, placed on a platform and carried around the town by four boys. It was an honor to be one of the four boys and I wanted very much to be selected. I was picked a couple of times and proudly lugged the platform and the beautiful statue of Mary through the rutted streets, the dusty back roads, the narrow alleys and into every corner of town so that everybody in Haina would have the privilege of seeing Mary. When such days were over, I felt better inside, as though made holier by my physical effort. I knew and, in a sense, worshipped Mary. Christ? Who was He?

It was only after I began reading the Bible from Roque that I found that the focal point of Christianity was Christ. I didn't want to admit that Christ had been missing from my life, but the more I read the more I knew that this was the case. This missing Christ of Christianity, I found, was the *only* means of salvation. Hebrews 10: 11, 12 (KJV) told me, "And every priest standeth daily ministering and offering oftentimes the same sacrifices, which can never take away sins: But this man (Jesus), after he had offered one sacrifice for sins for ever, sat down on the right hand of God. . . . "

I saw that Luke was referring to Christ when he wrote in Acts 4: 12 (KJV) that "Neither is there salvation in any other: for there is none other name under heaven given among men, whereby we must be saved."

And the words of John 3: 16 (KJV) radiated a new truth to me as I read them again and again: "For God so loved the world, that he gave his only begotten Son, that whosoever believeth in him should not perish, but have everlasting life."

I admire those who can see the simplicity of the Bible and its plan of salvation. I will not, however, blame anyone who does not understand. How could I blame anyone, when I myself did not understand for so many years? It is not easy to admit that you are a sinner, but it helps when you find that the Bible says that " . . . all have sinned, and come short of the glory of God." (Romans 3: 23, KJV.) In other words, we are all the same, all sinners, all getting ready for our boat to sink. He wants us only to confess our sins, to accept Christ and He will grant forgiveness, salvation and all His many gifts.

Perhaps the most troublesome part of all this talk about being a sinner is that most of us feel that we are decent people. We hear the word sin and we recoil and when we hear someone calling *us* a sinner we recoil even further. In the English language, sin is a strong, bold venomous word that is almost never used outside of a theological context. I have heard mothers call their mischievous children every name imaginable, yet I have never heard one call her child a sinner. Sin and sinner are imposing words in English. Sin, basically, is living outside the will of God, something that every one of us is guilty of even after we give ourselves to Christ.

Saint Paul, generally considered the saintliest of the saints, referred to himself as the "chief of sinners." How could this be? I have heard it likened to the case of the man who had a black smudge on his white shirt, and I think it is an apt analogy. As black as that smudge was, the man never noticed it as long as he remained at the end of the room where there was no light. When he walked over to the other side of the room and stood in the presence of a bright light, however, he immediately saw the smudge. Seeing the smudge and doing something about it are two different things.

Most of us tend to cling to that which we are, for we really don't understand what it means to accept Christ and to have salvation. Having no other experience we could possibly compare to this, our ultimate acceptance of Christ rests on faith. If *you,* perhaps for some reason you don't even understand, have faith that Christ was the Son of God and that He died for *your* sins, then it remains only for you to tell this to God and to give Christ entrance into *your* heart.

> " . . . if thou shalt confess with thy mouth the Lord Jesus,
> and shalt believe in thine heart that God hath raised him
> from the dead, thou shalt be saved" (Romans 10: 9, KJV).

A confession of our sins and an acceptance of Christ does not mean that we comprehend all that the Bible says, nor does it carry with it a guarantee that we will have full understanding within 30 days. At the time I got down on my knees in the clubhouse, I had been reading the Bible sporadically. I had been able to grasp certain truths, but that which I knew was far outweighed by the questions I had concerning that which I did not know. How could I accept Christ when I did not have all my questions answered? Only because I had a little bit of the same faith that all of us have when we flick on the light switch and are absolutely positive that light will follow at once even though all our questions about electricity will never be answered.

Al Worthington, the pitcher who helped me take my first step as a newborn Christian, did not abandon me in the bullrushes, choosing instead to nurture me in the word of God. Before the end of the 1958 season had come, the two of us had spent a number of hours together in praying, in studying the Bible, in just plain talking. There is still a vivid recollection of a trip we made to St. Louis to play the Cardinals, for it was on that trip that we got together every day at the hotel to pray. There is no way I can ever thank Al enough for his counseling during those trying days.

Having a friend like Roque waiting for me when I returned to the Dominican Republic was also fortunate. In my country almost everyone is Catholic. It was easy for me to realize why so many people resented my leaving the Church, but it was hard in some cases to convince people of the sincerity of my motives. There were some people who felt that I had abandoned the Catholic faith because I had become stuck up now that I had made the major leagues. I tried my best to convince them that it is hard to be terribly impressed with yourself when you have hit no more than .253.

There were arguments at home, too. My mother and other relatives kept telling me that all a person had to do to obtain salvation was to be a decent human being, that good works was all that I needed. I found it impossible to try to quote passages from the Bible, for these people, although they were firm Catholics, knew almost nothing about the Bible. As I spoke to these people I began to realize how deep my love for them was. I wanted desperately for them to understand, yet it was easy to see that the more I tried, the more antagonism I created. Almost everyone regards his religious convictions as a highly personal matter and, as important as the issue may be, often prefers not to exchange opinions.

There has been a considerable change in Catholic thinking in recent years and I can see that the Church is granting its members much more freedom in many areas. I know that in the Dominican Republic the Catholics do more Bible reading than years ago, that they no longer have to fear condemnation if they visit another church, that much of the fear of the Church and its hierarchy has been removed. I have been very happy to watch these changes come about. These are my people and I want only the best for them. I know several Catholics who have accepted Jesus and I feel that there soon will be many others now that they are looking into the Bible without fear of censure.

When some of my friends became angry with me because of my Christian stand, I tried to maintain the same understanding I witnessed in a woman who came to my home one day. She was a strong Christian who had heard about me and wanted to know if I would take a message to one of her sons in Chicago when I returned to America. When my mother found out that this woman was a Christian who shared my beliefs, she told her to leave the house. I'll never forget the calm expression on that lady's face and the sincerity in her voice as she said to my mother, "I will pray hard that you will understand." This may sound like the sort of statement that is used in a holier-than-thou way, but I saw the earnestness in the woman's eyes, could almost feel the compassion in her voice.

It is hard for my people to understand. There has always been so much unrest in our land. Ours is a country that occupies two-thirds of an island, the remaining one-third being the nation of Haiti. It was Christopher Columbus who discovered our land in 1492 and we are proud that he loved it above all those that he discovered. We are also proud that he named it Hispaniola in honor of Spain and that, although he died in his homeland, his remains were brought to Santo Domingo, in accordance with his will.

Shortly after Columbus landed in Hispaniola he engaged in a massive battle against the Indians who inhabited the island, killing many of them. Out of this clash came a saying that is still in use throughout the Dominican Republic: "A nation built on the blood of innocent people cannot have peace." That saying, unfortunately, has been absolutely correct. England, France and Spain squabbled over our country and after they got through with it along came the Haitians from across the border to conquer us. This was one of the lowest points in our history.

Our fight for independence began in 1844, a crusade begun by a small band of men of great courage, a crusade that others were soon to join until, at last, the Haitians had been driven away. That is a victory that inspires Dominicans to this day. When mention is made of what happened next, however, we have to turn our head in shame. Not long after they had gained their freedom, the people began fighting among themselves. That has been the history of my people: when they are not busy fighting off intruders, they are busy battling each other.

Ours is a poor country. We know it and the world knows it. But our country is also beautiful. She wears the sea as a necklace of shimmering blues, fingertipping into inlets to blend with the green-green of her complexion. Her early-morning sun gives you a wink, as though to steal your heart, if she hasn't already done so. I have been to numerous other countries and have found each to have a charm of its own, but in none have I found the striking beauty that exists right in my own land. Of this I am proud. I am not proud of the man-made ugliness that haunts my country—the poverty and politics that have scarred so deeply.

Precisely how bad Trujillo was for the Dominican Republic cannot be judged even now, more than five years following his assassination. Yes, he was a dictator and he committed atrocities against those who would not cooperate with him. He was also a leader who, although he could see his country writhing in poverty, would not let the people act like savages. During Trujillo's reign there was never any need to warn the people about being litter bugs, for no one would dare defy the General's edict on cleanliness. Alas, his fetish for cleanliness was not matched by his humanitarianism. He was cruel, often merciless, in his treatment of his fellow man.

Once, after Trujillo had a spat with Cuban officials, he issued a ruling that anyone caught listening to Cuban radio broadcasts would be jailed. Trujillo was able to enforce such edicts because he had a strong grip on every activity that went on within the country, thanks to his army of secret agents working for him. They were everywhere and if they caught you saying or doing anything against Trujillo it didn't matter how young or old you were, you were in serious trouble. It got so bad at one point that you couldn't be sure who was a spy and who wasn't and you had to be fearful of friends and family.

People were afraid, terribly afraid as long as Trujillo was in power, but I think most of them respected the high standards of personal conduct that he demanded of his people. After his assassination there came an almost immediate decline in the conduct of the people: garbage was piled in the streets, almost every exterior wall of every building was smeared with political slogans, many of the common courtesies of everyday life were thrust aside.

Years of open warfare were soon upon us. I recall fleeing with my family from Santo Domingo to Haina at about 9 o'clock one morning when fighter planes began strafing the city. Bullet holes are the pock-marked insignia of Santo Domingo. Now, I hope, my country is through with revolts. In the spring of 1966 a democratic election was held with Joaquin Balaguer, who had been ousted by a military coup in 1962, chosen president. Balaguer is the fruit of the bloody revolution of 1965, an argument that became a war, complete with tanks, hand grenades, intervention by thousands of American troops and the loss of some 2,500 lives.

Many people contend that this latest revolution was communist-inspired. It is quite possible that they are right. The communists have tried to take over the country before. I recall that when Fidel Castro was entrenched in the Sierra Maestra during his campaign to seize power in Cuba that he became a hero to me. In those days all Latin Americans were pulling for Castro, who was regarded as the good little guy trying to free his nation from the big bad guy. When Castro finally overthrew Fulgencio Batista, Latins everywhere celebrated as joyously as did the Cubans.

That was on January 1, 1959. On June 14, 1959 an invasion party came from Cuba to overthrow Trujillo. Suddenly we found that the same men we had been rooting for in the Sierra Maestra had landed in the Dominican Republic by plane and boat and were turning our country into a battleground. We didn't know which side to be on, whether to align with Castro, the people's hero, or with Trujillo, our iron-fisted dictator. Most of us backed Trujillo. Although he wiped out the invasion force, that clash was the beginning of the end for him. Many young people were captivated by the audacity of the invasion and they formed an organization called the 14th of June Movement, a revolutionary group that exists today with strong communist backing. Whether members of this faction actually provoked the 1965 revolt is hard to say. Communism took a bad beating during the election of 1966, yet there is no denying that it is a powerful factor in the behind-the-scenes political struggle that has become a part of the Dominican way of life.

Quite a few people have suggested to me that I move to the United States permanently so that I could escape the backwardness, the constant danger and the futility of life in the Dominican Republic. I do not intend to move, ever. A few years ago I read a book that pointed out that when the Haitians overran our nation, many of the finest families fled to Spain, Venezuela, the United States and elsewhere. As so often happens in such instances, those who remained were the poorest, the ones with the least talent and the least initiative—hardly the best cornerstones on which to rebuild a nation. There is a theory that one of the reasons for the constant feuding among Dominicans is because so many of them are illiterate and indifferent and because there are so few capable of really helping them. Much the same, I believe, has been true in Cuba, where such large numbers of good people have fled to other countries because they wanted to escape Castro. So many tens of thousands have left that there are not enough remaining in Cuba to even try to think of forming a united effort to save the country. At least for the time being, Cuba is without hope, a nation gripped by Castro and communism. I don't want this to ever happen to my country.

It is true that life in the Dominican Republic is like a variety of daily Russian roulette. It is not uncommon to see men and boys walking through the streets of Santo Domingo carrying pistols, rifles and submachine guns. At least four or five times I have been in the city when, without warning, shots started zinging through the air, showering the streets with splintering glass or whanging against the sides of buildings. When this happens, it is time to run for shelter or to simply drop to the ground and cover up your head. After the shooting is over, everyone gets up from the street or from behind wooden boxes or from under parked cars and business goes on as though nothing had happened.

Threats of communism, of another revolt and of being shot at are very real. Despite these dangers, I want to raise my children in the Dominican Republic, want to teach them the customs of our land and want to share with them the enjoyment of the good and beautiful things that *do* exist in our country. I want them to see the trees, now tall and green, that were planted along Independence Avenue by my mother's father when he was Trujillo's gardener. One of the most important steps that Dominicans must take, I feel, is to improve the strength of our family life. Too many youngsters are permitted to roam the streets, there to take part in fierce gang fights and vandalism. If we can bring up children to respect authority, to conduct themselves as decent men and women and to have a purpose in life, then we will have made a long stride toward getting our nation on a respectable footing.

Some people have told me that I should enter politics, but I seriously doubt that I would ever do this. To put it simply, I was not cut out to be a politician. I lack cunning, guile and the innate shrewdness to even start in politics and, furthermore, lack the education. Almost every college student in the Dominican Republic today is a politician, I am ashamed to say. All too often their politics consist of standing outside the government palace and demonstrating for one cause or another. These young people also spend a lot of time riding around in cars with loudspeakers, blaring out such news as, "Come to the rally tonight at the University" or "Come see the movie on Vietnam tonight." Innocent? Hardly. Many of these apparently harmless affairs are tools of the communists.

As for myself, my gifts are speed, coordination and physical, rather than political, power. In every nation there are doctors, merchants, lawyers, all playing vital roles in their society. I am nothing more than a ballplayer, but I can see that it is possible for me to help my nation, too. As a baseball player there is not much that I can do. As a player with Christian convictions, I feel there is something that I *can* do. When my playing days are over, there is nothing that I would enjoy doing more than working with youngsters. I feel they are especially in need of guidance just before and during their teenage years. Ideally, I would like to instruct them in physical education and baseball and would like to present my Christian testimony to them. Christ has helped me so much that I have to believe with all my heart that He can help others. Our country needs all the help it can get. It has been seeking a leader, never accepting the fact that Jesus, who has inspired more great leaders to more worthy deeds than anyone, has been available to them for all these years. One of the symbols on the Dominican flag is a Bible, an *open* Bible. I feel that if my people would open their Bibles they would find the answers to both their own needs and to those of our land.

CHAPTER

A "No" for Mr. Giles
and a
"No" for Mr. Rigney

That winter of 1958-59 was a pleasant one in spite of the difficulties of trying to make myself understood. Down to the sea, ever-faithful to give to me of her richness. Through the sugar cane fields, cutting a stalk and drinking the sweet juice. Into the mountains to enjoy a beauty that seemed to deepen almost from minute to minute. Running barefoot, throwing stones, making a slingshot and using pieces of coral for ammunition, watching the afternoon rain come and go as abruptly as if someone had turned a shower handle on, then off. And climbing the coconut trees.

There are two ways of climbing a coconut tree. If the tree is a straight one, it is best to wrap your arms and legs around the trunk as tightly as possible and then shinny all the way up. If the tree is angular, the fastest way to get to the top is to wrap your hands around the back of the tree, arch your back, plant your feet firmly on the trunk and literally walk your way up. After the coconuts have been knocked to the ground, they are cut open with a machete. First the thick outer shell is sliced off. Then a hole is cut in the top of the hard brown inner shell. This accomplished, you tilt your head back and drink of the cool and refreshing water that is inside. Coconut water is one of my favorite drinks, ranking right up there with orange juice. One day I drank the water—there is much, much more water in coconuts taken right from the tree than there is in those bought in super markets in America—from 11 coconuts. On another occasion, I filled myself to capacity by eating 45 oranges.

That winter I also found a new pastime. Ever since I had been a youngster I had heard and read about people who had done all sorts of exciting things in the sea—finding treasure, locating sunken ships, spearing fish. My imagination often ran away with such dreams, but I was always left far behind, a victim of reality. Then one day I met a man who said that since I was from Haina I must surely know where the best places to fish were. We walked down to the sea and I pointed out some spots to him. He put on a snorkeling outfit and fins, picked up his spearfishing gun and dived right into the heavy surf that my parents had always told me to avoid.

Back and forth, in and out he swam, and with a power and swiftness that made it seem as though he were in command of the sea. More than that, every few minutes he would raise aloft a large fish that he had caught. He was able to do this because his snorkle permitted him breath while he kept his head under water to search for fish. This was a display of fishing prowess that far exceeded anything I had ever seen before.

Below me the surf hurtled itself at the shoreline, sending sprays of blue-water-turned-white high into the air. Echoes of my parents' warnings crowded in on me. Finally, though, I could resist the temptation no longer and dived in. I had no snorkeling equipment, only a machete for trying to spear fish. It didn't take long to find out that fishing with a machete leaves much to be desired. As soon as I could, I hurried into town and bought myself a snorkeling outfit.

Soon my interest in what was going on beneath the surface of the sea turned to fascination. In the years since I first began this hobby I have gone snorkeling and scuba diving hundreds of times, for below the surface of the sea I have found a new world with a kaleidoscopic beauty all its own. Coral comes in all shapes and sizes, and dresses in only the loveliest colors. Branches of coral often jut out dainty arms, a sort of underwater filigree. No matter how often I submerge, I always seem to come across a variety of fish I have never seen before. Vegetation grows in profusion, sometimes arrayed in clusters resembling a garden, other times spread out here and there and at other times bunched together like an aquatic forest.

Within the sea all is quiet. No car horns, no squeal of brakes, no telephone jumping into my dreams. Eternal, restful silence dominates the sea. A fish swims by, the plants wave to the pulse of the sea, the coral stands guard—all silent. It is, in a word, relaxing.

That winter, as I had done in previous years, I played for the Escogido Reds in the Dominican League. Geographically, Escogido is a sector of Santo Domingo. Etymologically, Escogido means "the chosen" and alludes to the fact that the team was formed from the rosters of two others, with only the best players chosen for the new club. Prior to this the Licey team had dominated baseball in Santo Domingo. Since the merger of the two teams into one, Escogido has been the most powerful team in the Dominican League.

It was during that winter that I had the best season that I have ever had in the Dominican League. In all, I set seven league records, including one for the highest batting average (.359). I also set a mark for stolen bases with 19, which shows that, although my injury may have slowed me down, I still had a bit of speed. My home run total of nine was the most ever by a native player, but was far short of the record 14 hit the season before by Dick Stuart of the Aguilas team in Santiago. Salty Parker, a coach with the Giants, was my manager during that winter season and he brought our team home in first place. In the Dominican League the second- and third-place teams in the four-team league hold a five-game playoff to determine which one will go into the championship round. Licey, our big rival, not only won the playoff, but went on to upset us in the ninth-and-final game (our championship series is a best-of-nine affair) of the title round 3-2. Santo Domingo, always a city that expresses its feelings, expressed itself full-force. In this case, some 75,000 people marched and danced through the city streets to toast the Licey victory.

That loss was the only bad part of what was an almost perfect winter for me. What made it best of all was that a few weeks before going to spring training in 1959, Maria and I were married. One of the biggest blessings of my life has been to have a Christian wife for a partner. Before joining the Giants for spring training in Phoenix my feeling was that I was due to have a lucky season. After one season of having been dogged by the racial situation, another of being injured and a third of being called up from the minors before I was ready, I thought luck would be with me. In a way, I suppose that I expected the Lord to steer me away from turbulent waters, to give me a smooth ride. At that time I was not familiar with a passage of Scripture which says that " . . . tribulation worketh patience. . . . " (Romans 5: 3, KJV.) Before the season ended I had come to appreciate what those three words meant and could only conclude that the Lord was trying to make a patient man out of me, a very patient man.

Although accepting Christ had given me a greater inner peace than I had ever known before, I soon found that it does not mean that life will now go on troublefree. Instead of having less trouble than in the past I was finding out that standing up for my Christian beliefs got me into more tight corners than ever. As I look back, it is easy to see that there were reasons for this. Non-Christians sometimes were anxious to test me, to see how much I could take and to see how sincere I was in my convictions. There were other times when I got into awkward spots simply by standing up for what I felt was right.

My first bit of trouble came from a conversation I had with Orlando Pena, a Cuban pitcher who was with Cincinnati in those days. This was a violation of the major league rule against onfield fraternizing with players on opposing teams. I do not deny that I broke this rule. What I object to even now is that there is no flexibility in this ruling, no allowance, for example, that took into consideration the problems peculiar to Latins. Pena had only recently left his homeland and there was no going back, not with Castro sitting on high. Orlando had left behind his family, his friends—everything. Here, I thought, was a man in need and I wanted to talk over things with him to see what could be done. The league expects us to do our talking with opponents after games. This sounds very simple. It is not, because players on the road are usually resting either from their travels or a ball game. Players at home have their families to take care of. In short, things do not always go as smoothly as they should. Trying to explain this to National League officials in those days would have been like trying to teach a monkey to whistle *Dixie* with a mouthful of soda crackers.

Shortly after my chat with Pena, a telegram arrived from the president of the National League, Warren Giles, informing me that I had been a naughty boy and that my penance would cost $10. I bristled. They—the league and Giles—weren't going to get $10 out of me for doing what I felt was the right thing to do. Since there was no use trying to explain my side of the case—in such instances there is only one side, the league's—and since $10 was a lot of money to me in those days, I was determined not to pay. For the next few weeks each time I checked into a hotel in another city in our swing around the league, I had a friend waiting for me in the form of a telegram from Warren Giles. Eventually, probably because he had already sent me more than $10 worth of telegrams, Mr. Giles stopped sending me reminders. Now that the statute of limitations on such cases has expired I can admit all this and say that I have never paid that $10.

That run-in was one of the least of my problems in 1959. I had started off in spring training by getting a home run in my first at bat. My second time up I hit another homer. On my third try I singled and when I attempted to stretch it into a double I hurt my ankle sliding into second base. That, plus a heavy cold, put me on the sidelines for a few days. I also started off the regular season hitting well. In my first game of the year I hit a two-run homer in the ninth to help beat the Cardinals 6-3. During our first three home games in Seals Stadium I had six hits, including two home runs, in 11 times up and had picked up two stolen bases. For the month of April my batting average was .368 and I had four homers and 11 runs batted in. It looked like a good year. No sooner had my confidence started to go up than my batting average started to go down. It dropped under .270, with the result that I was being used only off and on.

Just when I thought that things couldn't get much worse they did. This was during the last week of July. It was the week that the Giants called up Willie McCovey and Jose Pagan from Phoenix. When I came into the clubhouse that afternoon I saw that my name had been taken off my locker and that Pagan's had been put up. I was shocked. When I asked what was going on, the only one who knew anything was the clubhouse man. "They're sending you down to Phoenix," he said, and then added, "By the way, Rigney wants to see you in his office."

I went right in to see Rigney. He said, "Felipe, we have a chance to win the pennant and we need McCovey and Pagan here to help us. Since you and Andre (Rodgers was also being sent down) aren't playing regularly, I think we'll send both of you down to Triple A until the season is over and then we'll bring you back up."

"Mr. Rigney," I said when he had finished, "I don't have much to say, except that I am not going to Phoenix." I told him that my wife was having a difficult pregnancy and that the weather would be too hot for her in Phoenix. Then I added: "Next year if you want me to play in Phoenix I'll play for you, but not this season. If you try to farm me out, I'll leave and go right home to the Dominican Republic." He was surprised both by what I had said and because I had spoken up. I was known as one of the quiet ones on the club. I knew that my defiance jeopardized my entire career, but I did what I felt had to be done to protect my wife.

After a pause Rigney said, "If that's the way you feel about things, you'll have to tell your story to Horace Stoneham."

Stoneham was the owner of the club, but I told Rigney that I would be happy to talk with him. After all, how often does a Triple A player, which is what the Giants figured I was, get to talk to the president of a major league club?

Rigney put in a call to Stoneham. There was no answer. Chub Feeney, a vice-president of the club as well as a nephew of Stoneham's, was available, however.

"What do you mean by this?" Feeney wanted to know. "Do you realize that if you go home at this point in the season it will cost you a couple thousand dollars in salary?"

"Yes," I said, "but money is not the answer to everything. I'd rather go home than risk the health of my wife and child."

I felt a little sorry for Feeney, an easy-going gentleman who didn't deserve to be put in such an awkward position. Still, I felt relieved at having had a chance to express myself. The next move was up to the Giants, I thought, as I went back to the apartment and talked things over with Maria. We were living in North Beach, a neighborhood known for its beatniks. Many a night or morning I would come home from a game or a road trip, the stars and moon well-lit and quiet above, the beatniks well-lit and noisy down below. They weren't too bad; just a group of people whose day began at 2 a.m.

The next day the headlines appeared in the newspapers and the stories told about my unwillingness to accept a demotion. McCovey took some of the heat off me by creating headlines of his own. In his first game for the Giants he went 4 for 4, hitting a pair of triples as well as two singles and accounting for five runs as the team whipped the Phillies 7-2. McCovey quickly entrenched himself at first base, with Cepeda moving first to third base and later to the outfield.

While McCovey was busy making a name for himself, I stayed at the apartment and packed up all our belongings. About the only thing I went outside for was to buy a pair of tickets for the Dominican Republic—one-way tickets. I had no assurance of any work except that I could play in the Dominican League starting near the end of October. Outside of that, the only thing I was sure of was my Christian faith.

Feeney sent the clubhouse man to the apartment to find out what was going on. He saw that everything was packed and, when he asked the obvious question, I told him we were leaving that night on a 10:20 flight. Feeney called me on the phone later in the day and said, "Okay kid, we're going to keep you. Get down here and put a uniform on."

The Giants did keep me, dropping another player to make room for me. It felt good to be back, but it was obvious from the start that Rigney was not pleased with my presence. He used me sparingly, letting me get up just 71 times during the final 60 games. I was almost useless as a pinch hitter, but after helping to win one game I recall that Rigney came over to me on the way to the clubhouse and said, "If I'd sent you to Phoenix we would never have won that one." I thought that was nice of him and it made me feel more like a member of the team than I had in weeks. My batting average picked up slightly in the last month and I finished at .275, with a total of just 10 home runs.

Although Rigney had little regard for me as a player, I feel he is one of the best managers in baseball. He was my first manager in the majors and when I came up as a rookie I didn't know how to evaluate him. Now I recognize him and respect him as one of the best. His gift was his ability to understand pitchers and to communicate with them. This is something that sounds simple. It is not. To handle pitchers properly a manager must master books on psychology, philosophy and weight control and, if he really wants to be well prepared, should commit to memory large segments of Dr. Spock.

Neither Rigney's understanding of pitchers nor our league-leading total of 165 homers was enough to earn us a pennant and we had to settle for third place, three games behind the Dodgers and Braves, who finished in a dead heat. The Dodgers beat the Braves in a playoff and then won the World Championship by stopping the Chicago White Sox in six games.

My downfall, as well as the failure of our team to win the pennant, gave me much to think about that winter. Not all of my sleepless nights could be attributed to baseball, however, for I became a father that winter and our first child, Felipe, Jr., sometimes decided that the proper time to eat breakfast was by the light of the moon. He was a joy, though, and when it came time to pack for spring training in 1960 we included him in our plans.

CHAPTER 9

SURVIVING A SLUMP AND TOKYO CAB RIDES

When I had first come up to the Giants some sportswriters had compared me to Willie Mays. Less than two years later, in the spring of 1960, they were comparing me to the many other promising young players who had never produced. I hadn't given up on myself yet, but my confidence was not what it used to be. Rigney had even less confidence in me than before. He started the season with Cepeda in left field and Kirkland in right and that was the way things remained until late in April. When Cepeda was hit in the head with a double play relay, I was finally given a chance to start and on April 29th I finally got my first hit of the year.

A week later Cepeda was back in the lineup and I was back on the bench, there to become well acquainted with every splinter as I sat and watched. When I did get a chance to pinch hit, I was futile. In one stretch of four turns as a pinch hitter I struck out, popped up, hit into a double play and struck out. One of my rare chances to start a game came on June 17th and it felt good to get a hit and contribute to a win over the Phillies. No sooner had I begun to have some hope that Rigney might keep me in the lineup than the news came the next day that he had been fired. In his place the Giants hired Tom (Clancy) Sheehan, a 66-year-old former minor league manager and friend of owner Horace Stoneham. It was a move that caught us by surprise. There was no denying that we had been slumping a bit, but we were still in second place just four games behind the Pirates.

Sheehan immediately announced that he was going to put Cepeda, who had been playing in left field, back on first base, a move prompted mainly by the fact that McCovey's batting average had fallen to .247. That made room for me in left field and in our first game under Sheehan I got my first extra-base hit of the season, a double. It wasn't long before Sheehan was experimenting. He put McCovey in at first base and when he failed again he tried Dale Long. Nothing seemed to work and the club kept losing game after game.

Before our game in Philadelphia on July 3rd, Sheehan gave us a tongue lashing, threatening us with fines, suspensions and demotions to the minor leagues. We went into that game having lost 12 of our past 17 contests and had fallen from half a game out of first place to six and one-half games back. That afternoon we tore into the Phillie pitchers and it was during that game, our 71st of the season, that I finally hit my first home run. There was no great turnabout in our performance, however, and we had to struggle for most of the season to stay above the .500 mark.

It had saddened me to see Rigney go so abruptly, but I was thankful that Sheehan was giving me the chance to play. It took me some time to get my batting eye sharpened, but at long last I was getting some hits that counted. There was one game late in July when I hit a hard smash to Milwaukee Shortstop Johnny Logan. He got his glove on it but couldn't hold it and it went for a single that gave us the winning run in the bottom of the 10th inning. It had been a long time since I had won a game.

I didn't really begin to hit the ball solidly until early in August in Pittsburgh, where two years earlier I had stopped hitting. My spree began when I went 5 for 8 in a doubleheader against the Pirates and it didn't end until a month later when I was hurt by a pitched ball. During that month I began to get some distance on my drives as I connected for six home runs and batted .363. About 10 days before I was injured I hit a home run off the left field foul pole for the first run scored off Milwaukee Pitcher Lou Burdette in 32 2/3 innings.

My finest moments of the season came in a three-game series against the Los Angeles Dodgers during the first week in September. This series began on a Friday night at Candlestick Park in San Francisco and it was in the seventh inning of the first game that I made possibly the best catch of my life. Tommy Davis was the batter and I was playing in deep left field to protect against his power. Instead of hitting the ball deep he hit it short and I had to come in at top speed, not daring to think I had a chance to make a play, yet hoping for the best. In desperation, I made a full-length dive for the ball, speared it in my glove and then had to make two quick somersaults to break my momentum and keep from injuring myself. That catch robbed Davis of a double and saved a 4-3 victory for us and Pitcher Jack Sanford.

That was the same game in which I had a pair of doubles and drove in two runs. It was a cold night for baseball, the temperature dropping into the low 50s. I can still see the umpires running into the dressing room or into the runway behind the dugout so they could rub their hands together and try to get warmed up before they had to go out for the start of another inning of play.

On the very next afternoon I hit a home run in the first inning off

Sandy Koufax. That was the only run of the game until the seventh inning, when the Dodgers put two runners on base and had Tommy Davis coming to bat. It was almost a carbon copy of the situation from the night before and when Davis hit the ball hard to left field again it seemed as though I had lived through all this once before. Again I made a diving catch to keep the ball from going through for a double. Our shortstop, Eddie Bressoud, made two spectacular catches of line drives that night. That was more than enough help for Mike McCormick—our ace lefthanded pitcher, not my former manager—and he hung on for a 1-0 win.

In the Sunday finale I hit a three-run, 400-foot homer through the infamous Candlestick wind and into the left field stands. A few innings later I came in fast to field a single by Jim Gilliam, then fired the ball to Catcher Tom Haller at home plate to cut down Charley Neal and the potential tying run. We went on to take that game by a score of 8-3.

Our combat with the Dodgers then shifted to Los Angeles and it was in the first inning of the first game there that Pitcher Stan Williams clipped me with one of his pitches and put me out of commission for 10 games. When I got back into the lineup, my timing was off and during the final two weeks of the season I hit a measly .164. My final average for the year was .264, not good, but a big improvement over the skimpy figure I owned until I had started hitting in early August.

Although we couldn't look forward to playing in the World Series, we were able to look ahead to a tour of Japan. It was an exotic-sounding trip that was to start with two games in Hawaii before going to Japan for 16 games. It was in the post-midnight darkness around the middle of October that we took off for Honolulu on the start of the most memorable road trip of my life.

In the first of our two games in Hawaii, Don Blasingame, Jim Davenport and I hit home runs as we won 5-1 against a team of civilian all-stars. Willie Mays hit a pair of three-run homers in the next game, but the big story was our pitchers. Stu Miller pitched six innings and did not allow a hit and then Sam Jones, Billy O'Dell and Billy Loes each added another hitless inning to wrap up a no-hitter and a 7-0 victory against an all-star team composed of servicemen.

Then it was off to Tokyo and the fabulous Orient. It didn't look fabulous when we got there, for Typhoon Mamie was on her way by to give Tokyo a wet kiss. We were greeted at the airport by Japanese dignitaries and kimono-clad girls, but as hard as everyone tried to be courteous and proper, strong winds swirled and slashed through the ceremonies. The most apt description of how bad the wind was came from one of our players, who said, "This is just like Candlestick Park."

Once we were past the official greeting ceremony, we all piled into 10 ancient convertibles for a ride to our hotel. We got caught in a traffic jam. It was not just an ordinary traffic jam. It was one of the worst in recorded history. We sat and waited and waited and sat and when we inched our way into downtown Tokyo we were bombed with confetti and ticker tape. There was no doubt that the Japanese people were friendly and enthusiastic, but the traffic jams they got into were almost beyond belief. I soon found out that the traffic snarl we were caught in was routine. Traffic, I found, moved well in Tokyo until it hit a bottleneck and then it seemed as though all the cars and buses and trucks were mired in lava.

Were it not for the inventiveness of the cab drivers, some of the jams would last for days. These enterprising cabbies would do *anything* to keep going, including driving up on the curb and driving on the wrong side of the road, two minor infractions that brought broad smiles to their faces as they urged their tiny cars up to 30-, 40-, 50-, 60-kilometers-an-hour. U-turns at such speeds are commonplace and are not preceded by any such thing as a hand signal or blinker. In Tokyo, it's every cabbie for himself in the scramble to get a fare. I am almost sure that the reason the Japanese people are so small is because they have to do so much running to dodge cars and that when they are not running off their weight they are busy worrying it off as they contemplate the horrors of the traffic that awaits them.

After having had a chance to observe cab drivers in several parts of the world I have a few conclusions to offer. Cabbies in America are, for the most part, not bad. They are inhibited by the law and the consequences of having an accident. In Tokyo they are suicidal. One tip when in Tokyo: avoid taxi drivers who wear gloves. These are the ones who believe that a firmer grip on the wheel means that they can make U-turns at 70-kilometers-an-hour rather than 60. In Caracas, Venezuela, the cabbies are involved in more wrecks than any place I've seen. They drive with malice aforethought. Taxi drivers in Santo Domingo are not without fault either. They drive with the same carefree abandon as the men in the demolition derbies. Stop signs are meaningless in the Dominican Republic, but in spite of the haphazard driving it is unusual to hear of any accidents.

Japanese ballplayers jolted us as much as the drivers did. In the first game of our tour before 30,000 fans in Korakuen Stadium in Tokyo, we lost to the Yomiuri Giants, the second-place team of the Japanese Central League. They had a left-hander named Ito who shut us out for six innings with a sharp curve. Somebody else came in to finish up the game for them as they beat us 1-0. It was in this game that I was thrown out trying to score from first base on a double to right field by Cepeda. Those Japanese showed us quite a bit and wrapped it all up by scoring the only run of the game on a squeeze bunt in the seventh inning.

It was not until the seventh inning of the second game that we scored our first run of the series. That run didn't help, for we lost 2-1. Starting with that game we played teams of all-stars for the remainder of our trip. After that loss we were assailed by the newspapers, which carried stories about our lack of determination and hustle. We didn't exactly cover ourselves with glory in the third game, but we did eke out a 1-0 win. Cepeda drove in Mays in the first inning and Juan Marichal protected that lead for seven innings. Billy O'Dell pitched the final two innings. It might not have been the most impressive of victories, but it got us untracked and we went on to win 10 of the final 13 games as we toured such cities as Sapporo, Osaka, Nagoya and Hiroshima.

One of the games we did not win wound up a 7-7 tie. That came on the day we got word that our new manager for the 1961 season was going to be Alvin Dark. We all felt relieved, for we had a great deal of respect for Dark even though he had never managed before. As ballplayers, we respected him for what he was: a hard-working, no-nonsense infielder who was tough in the clutch and who had an almost desperate desire to win. For half a dozen years he had been a standout shortstop for the Giants and in 1960 he had wound up his active playing career with the Phillies and Braves.

Sheehan gave us a talking-to before we went out for our game that day, telling us that we had been sloppy and lazy in our games so far and that there wasn't any excuse for it. We went out that day and got off to a 7-0 lead as Mays and Cepeda each hit two home runs and Andre Rodgers hit another. Those Japanese didn't give up, though, and they came back to tie us 7-7. After that we won seven games in a row. In the 15th game of our tour, a 14-2 win, both McCovey and I hit two homers apiece. The final game was a close contest. In the top of the ninth inning I hit a home run to put us ahead 2-1. The Japanese came right back, scored twice in the last of the ninth and beat us 3-2.

We finished up with a 11-4-1 record for the tour and with a total of 31 home runs. Before the series we were informed that the outstanding player would be awarded a Japanese car. I thought that McCovey was the leading player. He hit eight home runs and batted .423, the best figures any of us could produce. Mays had seven homers and a .393 average and was awarded the car. There is no denying that he had an excellent series, but you could almost predict, even before we began playing, that Willie would win the car. Being able to take pictures of Willie posing with the car meant a lot to Japanese publicity campaigns. Certainly nobody could help sell a car the way Willie could. Cepeda (five homers, .344) and Rodgers (.400) also hit very well. I ended up with four homers and a .308 average. The Japanese had also told us that the first player to hit a home run in each game would be given a radio. All subsequent homers, they said, would be worth boxes of candy. I couldn't develop the knack of hitting my home runs early, so I wound up without a radio and with four boxes of candy.

It had been a marvelous trip, complete with chances to dine on Japanese food, to dip ourselves into the bubbling inferno that the Japanese regard as their morning bath and to do plenty of sightseeing. We saw lots of Buddhas, temples and shrines and even played a game within clear view of Mt. Fuji. Perhaps the most captivating aspect of the whole trip was the people themselves. The Japanese are an industrious people who are never too busy to be polite. No matter how bad some of our performances on the field were, they never booed. I regard them as people with a great deal of class, big-leaguers all the way.

One of the most interesting asides to the trip was that it brought me into contact with the Fellowship of Christian Athletes for the first time. I'm still not certain how it all came about, but I do recall something about a letter from the FCA telling me that they had a representative in Japan who would be going from church to church explaining the workings of the organization. When I got to Tokyo a few representatives of the FCA contacted me and it was then that I learned that they wanted me to go with them to various churches to give brief talks. It turned out to be a laugh a minute. I was supplied with an interpreter and the poor man had to try to convert my mutilated English into Japanese so that the congregation could hear what I had to say. As I recall, I went to 11 such meetings. It was exciting for me to find that, in a land of Buddhas and Shinto shrines, there were people who knew and loved Jesus Christ just as I did.

When our final game and all our sightseeing were over, it was time to head for home. The process was not all that simple, however. According to arrangements that had been worked out ahead of time, we were to be split into two groups, one leaving immediately, the other lingering on for a few more days. After a year that included weeks of spring training, a 154-game schedule, road trips and a junket to Japan, we were in no mood to have to sit around any longer.

Booked on the first flight to America were all the big stars on the team, plus the front-office personnel. Cepeda and I were among those who were supposed to remain behind and we quickly expressed ourselves on the subject. It was decided that a drawing would be held, with all the names put into a box. Only a predetermined number could get on the first flight; the rest would have to wait. Eddie Brannick, the secretary of the club, did the drawing. The first name picked out of the box was mine. That trip home for me was unforgettable. I took a flight from Tokyo to Honolulu, changed to another flight for Los Angeles, then flew to San Francisco. After a stop in San Francisco, I took off for New York and then, finally, boarded a plane for Santo Domingo. It took me a day and a half to fly from Tokyo to home and by the time I got off the plane in Santo Domingo my legs felt like rubber. Honolulu had been beautiful, Tokyo enchanting, but when I got off the last plane and had a chance to look around, I concluded that there truly was no place like home.

The Dominican League season had been in progress for several weeks by the time I got home. My team, the Escogido Reds, had a 9-9 record and was in second place, two games out of first, before Juan Marichal and I were able to suit up. We won 20 of our last 30 games and took the pennant by four games. One of my teammates, Manny Mota, led the league with a .344 batting average. I hit .348 but was not entitled to the batting championship because I did not get enough at bats. My two brothers also hit well that season, Jesus winding up second in the batting race with a .330 average and Matty finishing sixth at .306. In the opening game of the playoff for the league championship the opposing pitcher walked Matty intentionally so he could pitch to me. I hit a grand slam homer and we went on to win that game and the title. It had taken me a long time to get my first hit of the 1960 season, but after I got stared I felt that I hit well enough in the National League, in Japan and in the Dominican Republic to give me encouragement for the 1961 campaign. More than ever I wanted to earn a job as a regular in the Giant lineup and I felt that I was really ready to do so. After having survived ordeals with Japanese cab drivers, I figured that there wasn't too much left that could frighten me.

CHAPTER  10

ALVIN AND
HIS CHIPMUNKS

Alvin Dark stood on the field on our first day of spring training in 1961 as the Arizona sun turned the park into a rotisserie. But Alvin Dark didn't seem to sweat. Maybe it was my imagination. Alvin Dark, though, definitely was different. He has become one of the most talked-about, controversial and respected men in the game and that was the spring that marked the beginning of the mystique about Alvin Dark, manager. Al has such a strong personality that many people who meet him for the first time are flabbergasted, some in a positive way, others in a negative way. For those who have any doubts about how to judge Dark, there are two rules of his life that should be weighed when analyzing the man: 1—every word, every action, no matter how illogical it may seem for the moment, has been well thought out; 2—Alvin Dark wants to win. To be sure, there have been times when, in the anger of the moment, he has violated rule No. 1. Never, though, has he swerved from rule No. 2.

I think that I might have been a little more anxious than anybody else to find out what sort of a manager Dark would be. This was because his home was in Lake Charles, Louisiana, where, during my brief stay in the Evangeline League, I had heard his name pop up in conversations daily and had seen it so often in the headlines of the local papers that even I recognized who he was. In the years since then I had played against him often in the National League. Now, however, Dark was back where he belonged, back with the Giant organization he had been a member of for half a dozen years. He had been named captain of the Giants during his playing days and had led the club to pennants in 1951 and 1954. Al batted .417 against the New York Yankees in the 1951 World Series. Three years later he was instrumental in the Giants' four-game sweep of the Cleveland Indians in the World Series, this time hitting .412. In Dark's day the Giants had been lodged in New York City. Since 1958, though, they had been in San Francisco, a powerful team, a disappointing team, a team in search of a leader. Alvin Dark was the leader they chose. They couldn't have made a better selection.

It took Dark hardly any time at all to make himself understood.

In one exhibition game against the Chicago Cubs, he had Ernie Banks, the slugging first baseman, walked intentionally. Walking Ernie Banks is acceptable strategy in most cases. But walking Ernie Banks or any other player during a spring training contest was something that was against baseball protocol. I can still hear fans and newsmen commenting about that move, saying that "after all, it's *only* an exhibition game." They might not have been interested in which team won, but Dark was showing us that he was interested and that he wanted his players to share in this quest for victory.

Al also told our pitchers to stop wasting time shagging fly balls in the outfield. Since they were never going to be used as outfielders, Dark told them, they might better spend their time taking batting practice, especially since a base hit here and there by a pitcher sometimes helps to win a game. Win. That's what Alvin Dark wanted us to do. Some people frowned on the idea of having Dark as a manager because he had never managed in the minor leagues. Most of the players felt that although there was a certain drawback to this lack of experience, Alvin possessed two plus factors that few other managers had: 1—having retired as a player only a few months earlier, he still retained the close communion with the game that he had known as a competitor; 2—he was a rarity among men—a born leader. Because he was endowed with this second quality, he was able to overcome any tendencies to convince us that he was a brilliant manager. He had the innate sense to know that if he tried to impress us he would actually repel us. Instead, he tried to use logic, hints, persuasiveness and encouragement, to which he invariably added his own telltale wink or slender smile.

Dark caused a few heads to spin with his dissertation on why a slow runner should be able to steal more bases than a fast one. Trying to impress upon us the need for more base stealing, Alvin explained that when a fast man was on the bases the opposition was always on the alert to keep him from stealing a base. Enter the tortoise-type runner. A lack of speed among the slower runners was an advantage, said Dark, and could best be exploited by getting a *late* start to steal second base. Late? Yes, late, said Alvin. Instead of tipping off the intent to steal, the slow man should delay longer than usual so that the second baseman and shortstop would have their full thoughts concentrated on the pitch being made to the batter. Now, with the second baseman and the shortstop getting a late move to cover the base, the catcher would be forced to hold up on his throw. Presto, a stolen base. It may be argued—it was in those days—that this idea is too far-fetched for any intelligent ballplayer to fall for. That may be entirely true, but the important thing was that Dark had made us

72

think about the art of stealing bases, about how to look for advantages and he now had us all talking and thinking baseball, which was his first goal.

After just a few days in his presence, I decided that Dark was a man who was going to live up to our expectation. I had heard that he was a strong Christian, but he was quick in letting me know that our oneness in faith would have no bearing on his attitude toward me as a ballplayer. Dark, a Baptist, told me that he himself had a rule against presenting his Christian testimony or preaching to any of the players while in uniform. It was a rule, Dark told me in unmistakable terms, that I was also to abide by. He told me that he felt there was ample time to talk about my beliefs but that while I was in the clubhouse and on the field I was to be dedicated to winning baseball games. I appreciated his forthrightness.

Al thought that I had the makings of a third baseman, so he gave me a trial at that position during spring training. It wasn't long before he told me that whatever makings I might have had, had somehow gone astray. When he dispatched me to the outfield once again I felt relieved. With Al playing each game for keeps, our club put together a 15-11 record during spring training, the third best mark for a National League team that year. We felt as though we were ready for the pennant race and that we had a legitimate chance to stop being the biggest perennial failure in baseball.

Our season began in Candlestick Park against the Pirates, who had perhaps signalled the beginning of the end of the Yankee dynasty by defeating the New Yorkers in the 1960 World Series. Dark used me as his leadoff batter and left fielder and I celebrated with a pair of hits. Our hitters, as usual, did quite a bit of celebrating, scoring seven runs. Our pitchers, as usual, struggled, weakened and finally succumbed. We had led by two runs with two men out in the top of the ninth inning, yet wound up losing 8-7.

In our next game, Dark took one of the many calculated gambles that he was to take that season. He felt that this was the moment to use Pitcher Billy Loes. There were several reasons why this was a risky choice. For one thing, Loes during the past two seasons had compiled a poor 7-9 record and an earned run average of well in excess of 4.00. Throughout his career he had also earned a reputation as one of the more eccentric players around, a talented temperamentalist who, when he wanted to, could pitch superbly. When he didn't feel in the mood to pitch, though, he didn't.

Added to Loes' own liabilities was the fact that Dark was skipping over other pitchers such as Mike McCormick, who had won 15 games the year before, and Jack Sanford, who had won a dozen games.

Also bypassed was Juan Marichal, who had come up from Tacoma in the Pacific Coast League the year before and had pitched excellently as he won half a dozen games in the final weeks of the season. All these more prominent pitchers had to rub their chin whiskers and wonder if Alvin Dark *knew* that this was going to be one of those days when Billy Loes would want to pitch. Then we all sat back and watched Loes muzzle the Pirates, one of the hardest-hitting teams in either league, as he picked up a 2-1 win. There were some who felt that Dark's masterful handling of Loes was surpassed by his influence on Cepeda. It was in the eighth inning that Cepeda let himself be hit by a pitch, a move that forced across what proved to be the winning run. No one likes to be hit with a pitch and after Cepeda allowed himself to be hit there were those who said that Orlando was beginning to be influenced by Dark's philosophy of victory at any cost.

Dark was busier than ever in our third game against Pittsburgh. We were trailing 4-3 in the eighth when he signalled for Mays to steal second base on the first pitch to McCovey, a lefthanded batter. (Dark later explained that, "A catcher has a harder time throwing to second base when a lefthanded batter is up.") After Mays had stolen second, Dark removed McCovey, who had now fulfilled his role as a cigar store Indian. Now batting for McCovey was Joey Amalfitano, a righthanded swinger. He wasted no time singling to right field to bring Mays around with the tying run. With Dark having one of his better days as a master manipulator, the Pirates were no match for us and we defeated them 6-5 in extra innings.

Dark was given a lot of credit for a lot of things and he deserved it. He also earned the nickname of The Mad Scientist from the press corps, a tribute to Dark's ability for making even the weirdest tactical maneuvers pay off. Our team became known as Alvin's Chipmunks. We were leading 2-0 in one game when Dark ordered a walk to Pancho Herrera of the Phillies. That put the possible winning run on base, a move that Dark survived when the next batter hit the ball right back to Pitcher Mike McCormick, who promptly threw the ball home for the start of a game-saving double play. Garry Schumacher, the director of public relations for our team, was so dazzled by the boldness and success of Dark's move that he stood up in the press box and announced, "I'm getting immersed in the morning. I'm turning Baptist."

One of the San Francisco sportswriters, concerned because Mays had not been hitting the ball well lately, had a talk with Willie before the game in Milwaukee on April 30th. "Don't worry about me," Willie told the writers, "I'll go out and get four hits today." Those four hits were really something—four home runs. It was quite a performance to watch as Willie became the ninth man in baseball history to hit four homers in one game. I hit one home run that day, hardly noteworthy except that it was one of a record-tying eight we had that day. We had hit five the day before and our two-day total of 13 was a new National League high.

A few weeks later, in a move that looked like an Alvin Dark Special, Mays scored all the way from first base on a single to left field. Willie, figuring correctly that the left fielder would throw the ball to the shortstop after fielding Cepeda's single, rounded second base at full speed and kept right on going for third. By the time that Phillie Shortstop Ruben Amaro realized what was going on, Mays was well on his way to home plate with an important run that helped us pick up a 4-2 victory.

Dark dropped me from the leadoff spot to No. 6 in the batting order shortly after the season began, hoping that I could get more runs batted in from that position. My average after almost three weeks was .326, but I hadn't had a single RBI. I picked up a few here and there and kept my average close to .300 for the month of May. My brother Matty, who had been brought up from Tacoma late in 1960, was now a member of the team and on May 15th against the Cubs we each hit a home run. A few days later we were playing the Cubs again and Matty got a pinch hit single to drive in the tying run in the eighth inning. That was the same game in which I scored the winning run in the 13th. Matty and I were starting to produce. We were a long way from being able to match the Boyer brothers—Ken of the Cardinals and Clete of the Yankees, two of the finest third basemen around—but we had the distinction of being on the same club. Sometimes the two of us wound up in the outfield at the same time. We began to laugh about the possibility of Jesus, who had also been signed by the Giants, coming up some day and thus putting all three Alous in the same outfield. That game in which I had scored in the 13th had been my first as a leadoff batter in several weeks and I had come through with three hits in six at bats. During my first nine games back in the No. 1 spot I hit .341. After being held hitless in my next game, I came back with three hits, including a two-run homer, that gave us a 4-2 win over the Dodgers and Stan Williams, the pitcher who had ended my spree the season before when he had hit me with a pitch.

We were winning games and held on to a slim lead in the pennant race throughout May. Winning half of our 30 games in June was not enough, though, and we slipped three and one-half games behind league-leading Cincinnati and a game back of Los Angeles. Alvin, the intrepid leader who had been given much credit for our early successes, now had to gird himself for the inevitable abuse that came his way once people learned that he was not infallible. I think it all began in a game in which Marichal, nursing a slim lead over the Dodgers, was removed in favor of Stu Miller. When Miller got into a jam and had a 2-0 count on Dodger Catcher John Roseboro, a lefthanded batter, Dark yanked Miller. In came Billy O'Dell, a lefthander, to pitch to Roseboro, who homered and gave the Dodgers an 8-7 triumph.

And now it is time to recount the strangest five-game series I have ever taken part in. All the games were played in Connie Mack Stadium in Philadelphia. The first game, a 1-0 loss in which we outhit the Phillies 8-4 but left a dozen men on base, was played in a steady drizzle. That was our sixth loss in eight games on our road trip and when Dark got to the clubhouse after it was all over he picked up a metal stool and threw it. What damage the stool did to the lockerroom I don't know, but I do know that it tore the end off the little finger of Dark's right hand. His pinky had somehow slipped inside a tubular piece of metal on the chair and thus, although Alvin let go of the stool when he threw it, the stool did not let go of Alvin. Frank Bowman, our team trainer, salvaged the tip of Dark's finger and put it on display in a bottle of alcohol. There was an awful lot of publicity given to this incident, but Dark took it well and the whole affair seemed to give just about everybody a chuckle. It also provided the newsmen, who now had proof that Dark had blood just like the rest of us, with evidence that Alvin was, indeed, human.

Our second game was almost too uneventful to be true. We led 12-0 going into the ninth inning and even though the Phillies scored five times we held on to win. What those last-place Philadelphians did to us the next day, however, was unconstitutional. There was nothing wrong with the score being tied 3-3 after nine innings. We didn't mind too much that they came back in the bottom of the seventh to tie us or that they did the same thing in the 13th. The 15th inning was what sent us away mumbling to ourselves. Jose Pagan hit a home run in the top half of the inning and we went on to add another pair of runs, giving us a safe 7-4 lead.

With Jack Sanford, one of our more dependable pitchers, on the mound, there seemed to be no way we could lose this game. We didn't lose, even though we tried very hard to. Sanford gave up a single, a walk and then run-scoring hits to Tony Gonzalez and Tony Taylor. That made the score 7-6 and left the Phillies with runners on first and third. With Catcher Clay Dalrymple, a lefthanded batter, due up, Dark brought in Lefthander Mike McCormick to pitch. There

76

were two outs at the time. McCormick got Dalrymple to ground out to end the inning. We therefore won the game, right? Wrong. Before getting Dalrymple out, McCormick had stooped down to finger the resin bag and while he wasn't looking Catcher Hobie Landrith had thrown the ball over Mike's head and into short center field. Before Pagan, our shortstop, could retrieve the ball, Gonzalez had scored with the tying run. There was a league rule prohibiting the start of any inning of a night game after 12:50 a.m. and since it was already beyond that time the contest ended. Thus it was that after five hours and 11 minutes—the longest night game ever played—we had to settle for a 7-7 tie. Worse yet, the whole game would have to be replayed as part of a twi-night doubleheader the next day.

Both managers—Dark and Philadelpha's Gene Mauch—refused to announce their starting pitchers before the first game. It was a fit of pique that was a prelude to another strange contest. When the lineups were turned in, O'Dell, one of our top relief pitchers, was listed as our starter. That was nothing compared to what Mauch was up to. He had five pitchers in his original lineup. Before the first inning was over, though, Mauch had replaced every one of them, including Starter Ken Lehman, who was allowed to face just two batters. That was one more than Dark let O'Dell pitch to. After O'Dell had given up a single to leadoff man Bobby Del Greco, Dark, according to preconceived strategy, brought in Sam Jones to replace him.

Dalrymple, who had been at bat when the Phillies had scored the tying run in the 15th inning earlier in the day, came right back to haunt us in his first trip to the plate in the opening game. This time he hit a routine ground ball that we thought we had turned into an inning-ending double play. Our team was halfway to the dugout before anyone realized that the umpire had ruled that we had missed the out at second base. In the mad scramble that followed, players from both teams raced pell mell around the infield. By the time we were able to retrieve the ball the Phillies had scored two runs. Mays had a single, double, triple, three homers and seven runs batted in that day, but because of the buffoonery that had now become a part of our style we didn't have an easy time winning. Willie's home runs all came in the opening game and it was his final one, which came in the 10th inning, that gave us an 8-7 win. It was the only satisfaction we could claim after having battled the Phillies for 25 innings.

The second game was so normal that it seemed abnormal. Loes was our starting pitcher and he went all the way, pitching a five-hitter for a 4-1 victory. About the only unusual aspect about Loes' performance was that he had pitched in relief during the first game and had looked bad, facing five batters and letting three of them reach base. Philadelphia fans, who are the most belligerent in the league, took exception to an umpire when he ejected Phillie Catcher Jim Coker from the game. They threw well over 100 beer cans, not all of them empty, onto the field during their sixth-inning outburst. We were glad to get out of Philadelphia.

Our sweep of the doubleheader against the Phillies had moved us past Los Angeles into second place and had left us just two and a half games in back of Cincinnati. Less than three weeks later, though, we had fallen to fourth place and were nine and a half games behind the Reds. We were still the sort of team that could beat the Cubs 19-3 one day and then turn around and lose by scores such as 3-2 and 2-1. I was having somewhat of a letdown after my good start. Matty was going well and there were times when he took my job away from me. I spent most of July on the bench and when I did get a chance to start a game there just weren't any hits in my bat.

Dark, though, had plenty of tricks in his bag. One of his more interesting psychological moves came late in July when he sent Marichal out to face the Pirates. Marichal, who had failed to complete any of his past six starts, was told by Dark that, by golly, he would have to go all the way this time. "There's not going to be anyone in the bullpen to help you out," Dark explained to Juan. A properly motivated—frightened might be a better description—Marichal then went out, struck out six of the first nine men he faced and finished up with a five-hit shutout. Dark gave Sanford and McCormick the same "no bullpen" lecture he had given Marichal. Prior to this, these three starting pitchers had only 13 complete games in 54 starts. In five of their next six starts they went all the way, with the one exception being Sanford, who was removed in the 10th inning.

Not all of Dark's ideas met with such success. Less than a month after he had lost part of his pinky in Philadelphia, Alvin lost his temper again. This took place in the midst of our sixth straight defeat. When Cepeda was called out on strikes in the ninth inning, Dark objected and did so in person. Dark, whose language is usually faultless, got in a few purple words to Umpire Shag Crawford, who christened Alvin by ejecting him from his first ball game since taking over as manager.

Dark was quoted the next day by Prescott Sullivan of the *San Francisco Examiner* as saying that, "My wife, Adrienne, says I should be ashamed of myself and I thoroughly agree. It wasn't a Christian thing to do. It was Satan's work. The devil was in me. Never before have I so addressed any man—and, with the Lord's help, I hope to have the strength never to do so again. Crawford is a fine man and a fine umpire. It was doubly wrong to say to him what I wouldn't willfully say to the worst of men. . . . It's a long season and all of us are sinners. Faith is our salvation."

I thought Alvin did an excellent job of expressing himself, pointing out in the process that being a Christian does not mean that we are going to be rid of pitfalls, worry or even ourselves. So many people seem to misunderstand this. They feel that we give ourselves to Christ because it will mean easy lives for us. It is true that the more we give of ourselves to Him the more peace we will have, for there will be less of our own will being exhibited in our lives. We will always retain our human nature, however, and it will repeatedly get us into trouble.

Other people have misinterpreted our belief in another way, feeling that we have accepted Christ because we want to be successful. They have heard Christian athletes say that they owe all their success to the Lord. What they are saying is that without Him they would have been nothing; with Him they have overcome themselves and gone on to accomplish things they could never have achieved alone. If accepting Christ meant success, then just about everyone would accept. Christianity is not founded on success, because too many insincere people would profess a love for Christ which they do not have. Christianity is founded on faith and it is a challenge, rather than a ticket to instant success, that a person accepts when he steps forward to commit his life to Christ. It has been said that faith can move mountains. I haven't see any mountains moved lately, but I have seen lives changed marvelously as men have, in simple faith, given themselves to Jesus Christ.

Success was one thing I was not having much of during July. Matty, though, was hitting even better than before and was holding down my job. He was involved in one of the oddest plays of the year, a pop-up to Chicago First Baseman Ernie Banks. There was one out and the bases were loaded, so the umpire called the infield fly rule. Then the Candlestick wind took over, giving Banks fits as he chased after the pop-up. He finally got his glove on the ball, but it glanced away for an error and a run scored. What made this such an oddity was that this was the second time that we had scored on an infield fly, both times against the Cubs. The first instance came earlier in the year and took place in Chicago. Ed Bailey, our catcher, hit a pop-up behind second base with the bases loaded one day. It was ruled an infield fly, but after the catch had been made Mays dashed from third base for home. Willie crunched into the Chicago catcher, sending him sprawling in one direction and sending the ball rolling in another. McCovey took advantage of the situation and scored, too, giving Bailey two runs batted in on an infield fly.

My first big day in months came early in August when I went

3 for 5, scored three runs, drove in four and had two homers as we won in Los Angeles 6-0. Marichal pitched a one-hitter, giving up only a single in the fifth inning to Tommy Davis. My average was down in the low .270s at this time and it didn't start to climb much until we played the Dodgers again, during the latter part of August in San Francisco. I had an almost exact duplicate of my big game against them two weeks earlier, getting 3 hits in 5 at bats, driving in four runs and hitting two homers. After a brief lull, I got off on another hot streak—it started against the Dodgers, naturally—and for the final four weeks everything went right. I hit a 10th-inning game-winning home run off ElRoy Face of the Pirates, went 4 for 4 and had four runs batted in against the Cubs and brought my home run total up to 18. For most of the month Dark had me batting either fourth or fifth.

One of my most satisfying games of the year came in Pittsburgh during the final week. Matty went 4 for 5, I went 3 for 5 and between the two of us we accounted for all the Giant runs in a 7-4 victory. During those last four weeks I picked up 34 hits and batted .386. That left me with a final average of .289 for the season. Matty outhit me, winding up with a .310 average in his rookie year. Jesus, in his first full year as a professional, batted .352, hit 11 homers and drove in 91 runs for Artesia of the Class D Sophomore League. He was moved up to Eugene in the Class B Northwest League at the end of the season and in six games there he hit .350.

Cincinnati, which clinched its first pennant in 21 years during the final week of play, finished four games in front of the Dodgers and eight ahead of us.

Matty and Jesus kept right on hitting in the Dominican League after the National League season ended and it was a shame that the season had to be called off after just one month of competition. Political tensions were running high since Trujillo's assassination on May 30th and that, plus a nationwide transportation strike, led to the shutdown of the league. Mob violence was becoming almost commonplace and groups of American players who were stranded outside of Santo Domingo were warned to stay in their hotel rooms. After two days, Manager Don Hoak of the Santiago club risked a get-away. Together with a group of his players—Donn Clendenon, Art Swanson, Larry Foss and Hal Jones—he took off for Santo Domingo in a car owned by one of the native members of the team. They arrived safely, thanks to a supporting task force that included a half-track that drove before their car and a jeep that brought up the rear. Both of these protective vehicles were equipped with heavy machine guns. Ford Frick, who feared for the safety of U.S. players, had cabled Hoak to evacuate himself and as many other U.S. athletes as soon as possible. By exercising the utmost ingenuity and boldness, Hoak led 11 Americans back home. Another cluster of players from the Licey club talked a cab driver into trying to get them to Santo Domingo. On the outskirts of the city they were stopped by a horde of angry taxi drivers who were on strike. They got out knives and slashed all the tires on the cab. There were six players in that forlorn group, but they managed to get a ride aboard a wagon and got into the city that way.

Shortly before the season was cut short I hurt my right leg again. I was hitting .349 at the time and had 19 runs batted in during our first 13 games. Jesus was hitting .293 and had 15 RBIs when the season ended with our team already four games in front. Matty, however, led the league in batting with a gaudy .408, plus 15 runs driven in. It became a long, tense winter with the sound of gunfire liable to come from any direction and at any moment. A 6 p.m. curfew was strictly enforced. Anyone caught outside his home after that hour was taking his life in his hands. My heart ached for my land and for my people.

CHAPTER *11*

THE "JAMMER"

While I was home in the Dominican Republic after the 1961 season, I did something very important: I began thinking about how I could improve as a ballplayer. Oh, I had given it some thought in past years. This time, though, I had just completed my finest season in the majors and still was not satisfied with myself. I wanted to figure out why I hadn't been able to hit for a higher average and with more power. After much thought, I felt I had come up with the right answer. I finally realized that there was just one person who was hindering my progress—me. I was guilty, I admitted at last, of actually helping the pitchers get me out. This was something that I had been vaguely aware of, but I had never been willing to admit to myself.

Now that I had brushed aside enough of my pride to get a clear look at myself, I could see that I had been giving in to the pitchers because of a fear of the "jammer." This was the name given to the inside pitch, which was being used more and more to tell the batter that if he didn't back away from the plate he would soon be a mass of bruises. I now could see that the pitchers had done a good job of jamming me and, consequently, instilling fear. (It's not cowardice so much as it is a fear for your career. Neither I nor any other player *wants* to be hit by a pitch, for you can be hurt and possibly sidelined. We get paid for playing, not for sitting on the bench.)

I knew that the pitchers were on to my ability to hit the curveball and that they were getting me out mainly with fastballs and sliders. Making an out is bad enough, but the way the pitchers were setting me up was what hurt most. Because of my respect for the jammer, I had been using a wide-open batting stance, planting my left foot far from home plate and my right foot close to the rear of the plate. This stance made it easy for me to move out of the way of pitches that came in close to me. It also made it easy for pitchers to keep me unsettled by throwing fastballs on the inside of the plate. Having driven me away from the plate, they would then polish me off with a slider, a pitch that would appear to be coming in tight once again but which would break away from me at the last instant. Too many pitchers were aware of how to set me up and they were making me look ridiculous.

Having at last placed the blame where it belonged, it was up to me to decide whether I wanted to keep playing it safe or whether I was ready to show the pitchers who was boss. I decided to stop giving in to the pitchers, and during the brief Dominican League season that fall I tried to correct the flaws in my batting style. What I did was to move my left foot closer to the plate and my right foot further away. This made me vulnerable to inside pitches and it meant that, if I wasn't going to back off from them, I would have to hit the ball before it got on top of me. It meant I would have to be more aggressive, that I would have to attack the ball. Since making this adjustment I have been a better hitter than ever before. Using my new batting stance and my new attitude about attacking the ball, I hit .461 during spring training in 1962. I could hardly wait for the regular season to get under way so that I could find out if my new batting technique was really going to pay off.

We opened the season at home against the Milwaukee Braves, who used Warren Spahn that day. I got two hits off Spahn, but that didn't prove anything to me because I always had done well against him. Mays, who also hit Spahn well and who, 11 years earlier, had tagged him for the first home run of his career, smashed Warren's first pitch of the season to him for a homer. We considered that a good omen, for the last time that Willie had homered on Opening Day had been in 1954, the year the Giants had last won a pennant. Marichal made the day complete by giving up just three singles and we won 6-0. O'Dell gave up four hits the next day and we won again, 3-1. For the second day in a row, Mays hit the first pitch thrown to him for a homer, this time victimizing Carlton Willey. We told Willie that if he could keep up that pace for the next 160 games we just might win the pennant that we had been reaching for and always missing.

Willie let us down, however. He didn't get a home run in our next game. Still, we kept on winning. Cepeda and I each hit two homers in our fifth straight win, a 13-6 victory over Cincinnati. Above the scoreboard in left field at Crosley Field is a large clock and on top of that is a sign that reads OFFICIAL WATCH. One of my homers that day broke the W in that sign, which is 50 feet above ground level and 328 feet from home plate. Frank Robinson of the Reds broke up our winning streak by twice robbing Jim Davenport of extra-base hits. We came right back to take our next game by whipping the Dodgers 19-8. Facing Stan Williams that night, I hit one of the longest home runs of my career. It cleared the center field fence and landed an estimated 450 feet from home plate. One disenchanted Dodger rooter sent a telegram to our team that read:

ROSES ARE RED, VIOLETS ARE BLUE,
WE'LL GIVE OUR TEAM FOR FELIPE ALOU.

What was even more flattering than that was my hitting safely in each of our first dozen games. I also padded my .438 batting average with four homers and 14 runs batted in. Although we had an 8-4 record at that point, we were in third place. The St. Louis Cardinals must have been even more frustrated than we were. They had a 7-0 record and were second to the Pirates, who tied the major league mark by winning their first 10 games.

We took over the league lead on May 1st by beating the Pirates 4-2 for our seventh consecutive win. Little by little we were gaining confidence in ourselves as a team. When we defeated the Cubs 11-6 on May 4th, after having been up until 5 in the morning because of plane trouble, we began to feel that nothing could stop us. The next day the Cubs ended our 10-game winning streak and we realized that winning the pennant would not be a simple task.

One of the men who kept us going was Billy Pierce, a lefthanded pitcher we had picked up from the Chicago White Sox. Before the season began it was hard to hold out much hope for Billy, a 35-year-old whose earned-run average of 16.54 during spring training looked like the national debt. Once the season started, however, Pierce really showed us something. After four weeks he had a 4-0 record and a 1.74 earned-run average. Billy O'Dell was another pitcher who took his lumps from the preseason critics. He had won 14 games when he was with Baltimore in the American League in 1958 and now some people were down on him because he had won fewer and fewer games each year since then, hitting a low of seven for the Giants in 1961. O'Dell started the 1962 season by winning his first five games. He really silenced his critics with his fifth win, a 6-0 shutout in St. Louis, which he achieved despite swirling gusts of wind that reached more than 40 miles an hour. Billy gave up just four singles that night and contributed to our offense with two hits of his own. Not even his detractors could complain that he retired only 26 batters instead of the regulation 27. O'Dell got away with that thanks to a heavy rainstorm that swept over the field after he had retired the first two Cardinals in the bottom of the ninth inning.

Late in May the Mets came to San Francisco and we took three straight from them, though not without incident and not with ease. It took a two-run homer in the 10th by Mays for us to win the first game 7-6. Our second victory was by a 7-1 score and Mays starred again, winning the feature bout of the afternoon when he settled a dispute with Met Shortstop Elio Chacon by picking him up bodily and slamming him to the ground. There were many facets to the fisticuffs that took place that day. It all began when Mays was on second and Cepeda, who had been hit in the back by one of Roger Craig's pitches, was on his way to first. Cepeda had started for first, then made a sharp left and headed for the mound to take on Craig. Al Dark, who had been a football player at Louisiana State University, raced out of our dugout and stopped Cepeda with a flying tackle. Cepeda, properly subdued, took his place at first base. He was immediately picked off by Craig but was safe when First Baseman Ed Bouchee dropped the throw. Craig then tried to pick Mays off second. Mays slid back safely, spiking Chacon in the process. Chacon then slugged Willie, who hoisted him in the air and threw him to the ground. While that fight was going on, Cepeda once again headed for Craig and took a few pokes at him. Within seconds, everybody was milling around throwing vicious scowls at each other.

I'm certain that Mays and Cepeda enjoyed themselves that day. So did I, for I had five hits and six runs batted in during that Sunday doubleheader-brawl. The Mets almost had us in the second game until they came through with some of their usual clutch mistakes. We went into the eighth inning trailing 5-2. I recall getting a single that drove in our second and third runs of the inning, tying the score. Then I moved to third on a wild pitch and a stolen base. Although McCovey struck out, I was able to score the winning run when the third strike got by Met Catcher Harry Chiti.

Within the next week we swept two more doubleheaders, one in Philadelphia, the other in New York. At that point, we held a game and a half lead over the Dodgers. The date was June 2nd. Mays was batting .310 and had 18 home runs and 45 runs batted in after 54 games. Cepeda had 15 homers, 52 runs batted in and a .344 average. I had 6 home runs, 39 RBIs and a .346 average. Now that I was taking a solid cut at those inside pitches and pulling them down the left field line, I had taken away the effectiveness of the jammer. It was the pitchers who now had to be fearful when they decided to pitch me on the inside.

We moved along smoothly for a few more days, then lost twice to the Cubs by scores of 4-3, and twice more to the Cardinals by identical 8-4 scores. Two more losses to the Cardinals dropped us two and a half games behind the Dodgers. In mid-June, Pierce was spiked badly in the first inning of a game in Cincinnati and had to be taken to the hospital. It took a dozen stitches to sew up Billy, who had an 8-1 record at the time. Cepeda was hurt the next day when he tried to score standing up, crashed into Cardinal Catcher Gene Oliver and suffered a bad bruise and a Charley horse. With Cepeda out of action for our next game, Dark moved me into the cleanup spot. In my first time up I hit a two-run homer that helped Marichal gain his 10th win, a two-hit shutout of the Cardinals. A few days later the Braves beat us 11-9 in the longest nine-inning game ever played, a farce that dragged on for four hours and two minutes. That defeat dropped us two and a half games behind the Dodgers, but we regained the lead four days later after beating the Reds 6-5 in 10 innings. I sat out the game because of a sore shoulder, then came in to run for McCovey in the 10th. When Cepeda came through with a single, I decided to try to make it home all the way from first and I just did manage to slide in under the tag. In the final game before the first All-Star Game in early July, Sandy Koufax, with ninth-inning relief from Don Drysdale, shut us out 2-0 on three hits to move Los Angeles half a game ahead of us. It was shaping up as a two-team race between the Dodgers and us.

I was selected to the National League All-Star team that year, though not as a starter. Roberto Clemente of Pittsburgh beat me out for the right field job. At the time of the first All-Star Game, which was played in the new District of Columbia Stadium in Washington, Clemente was third in the league in batting with a .342 average and I was fourth at .328. I managed to get into the game for a few innings as Clemente's replacement in right field and also had one at bat. Dick Donovan of the Chicago White Sox was pitching when I came up in the eighth inning with Maury Wills of the Dodgers on third base. The best I could do was to hit a fairly deep foul to right field. Wills made the most of it, though, and turning on his speed, he beat the throw to the plate. That gave the National League a 3-1 lead and that's the way the game wound up. Cepeda had driven in one of our other runs and Marichal was credited with the victory. Now that we had helped the National League as best we could, it was time to plunge back into the pennant race.

Three losses in our first four games after the All-Star break enabled the Dodgers to pick up another length on us in the standings. It was the Mets who gave us our third loss, or rather we gave them the win. Whatever it was, we didn't look good. In the first inning of our next game against New York we didn't start out any better, largely because Met Outfielder Richie Ashburn kept getting in our way. Ashburn, well known for his Mother Hubbard arm, threw out Mays, well known for his prowess on the basepaths, when he tried to stretch a single into a double. In the bottom of the inning, Ashburn was caught in a rundown between third and home but wormed his way out of it when Jim Davenport, our usually alert third baseman, tagged Umpire Frank Walsh instead of Ashburn. This nonsense had gone far enough, so we went out and got 16 hits in the next eight innings.

I scored one of our runs when I came all the way around from second base on an infield out. That was pretty good base running, but it seemed like just another run as we built up a 9-2 lead. As it turned out, it was a big run, for we had to hang on to salvage a 9-8 victory.

Back in June I had been forced to leave the field in the middle of one of our games because of soreness in my right elbow. There were bone chips floating around in that elbow and it remained badly swollen for most of the season and caused me to miss a number of games. It also hampered my swing and during one stretch in late July and early August I had only one hit in 14 times at bat. Baseball, however, is not a game in which you can afford the luxury of a few extra days off to recuperate. My injury was an old one and, although I cannot prove it, my theory is that it came from the heavy work I did in my father's blacksmith shop. When I was 12 years old I was shoeing horses and doing a man's work. I was glad to be able to help out, but even then there was a pain in my elbow that wouldn't go away. The soreness in my elbow was one thing, but the soreness and numbness that struck Sandy Koufax of the Dodgers in mid-July was something else. Koufax came down with a mysterious ailment that brought numbness to his left hand and sidelined him until late in September. At the time of his misfortune Koufax had won 14 games. He was not to win another game the remainder of the year.

While we were dawdling around winning a few and losing a few, Los Angeles moved steadily forward. Five times the Dodgers put together four-game winning streaks and their overall record from July 12th through August 9th was 21-6. Even without Koufax (he won the July 12th game, his last before being disabled) the Dodgers kept winning. Drysdale won six games during that period, leaving him with a 21-4 record. Johnny Podres won five times, Williams added four victories and the bullpen combination of Ed Roebuck and Larry Sherry accounted for the remaining five. After the games of August 9th the standings showed clearly how bad off we were:

	Won	Lost	GB
Los Angeles	79	37	—
San Francisco	73	42	5½

We were now further behind than we had been at any other point in the season. With Pierce recovered from his spike wound, however, our pitching had begun to pick up. What's more, our hitting was showing signs of reviving from its mid-season slump. The Dodgers were coming to town for three games and we felt ready. Just to make sure, Dark gave special orders to the groundskeepers on how he wanted the infield readied for the Dodgers. When they came into Candlestick Park they had to contend not only with us, but also with

Beatle-length infield grass and watered-down basepaths, both designed to curtail the fabled Dodger speed.

The Dodgers howled and complained. (I would have, too, had I been on their club.) In a retaliatory move, the Dodgers stole our leaded practice bat. Not to be outdone, we stole *their* leaded practice bat. Both teams were even as far as thievery went, but where it counted most—on the field—we came out on top. O'Dell, Pierce, Marichal and Reliefer Stu Miller all pitched well and the hitters produced 21 runs. I accounted for three runs in each game and had eight hits in 12 trips to the plate. It all added up to three important victories.

September, the final month of the season, came and we still trailed Los Angeles by two and a half games. We promptly increased this deficit by another full game when we opened the month with a loss and the Dodgers started off with a win. On the 2nd of September the Dodgers won again and as we went into the last of the ninth inning of a tie game against the Reds we knew that if we lost it could be fatal to our pennant chances. We got a man on base and I hit a homer off Jim Brosnan that gave us the victory and kept us from falling further behind. Then we went to Los Angeles for a four-game series, knowing that we would have to take three of the games if we were to make a dent in the apparently armor-plated Dodger lead.

This time it was the Dodgers and their fans who made some special preparations for this series. Hundreds of Dodger supporters came to Chavez Ravine with duck calls, duck feathers and even a few live ducks, all of which was their way of mocking our watering-down tactics in San Francisco. On the steps in our dugout was a pink watering can on which was written a note to Catcher Ed Bailey. It said:

ED BAILEY'S
CHAVEZ RAVINE
1ST BASE
WATERING CAN

A live chicken and a live duck were thrown on the field during the first game. Nothing bothered Jack Sanford, though, as he earned his 20th win of the year—and 14th in a row—for us. The Dodgers, unhampered by a wet turf, took the next game 5-4. Willie Davis challenged Mays' arm and won, scoring all the way from first on a single to center. When Pierce took too much time with his windup, Dodger John Roseboro took advantage and stole home. After the first two games of the series we were worse off than our split indicated because we had lost two precious days and hadn't picked up an inch.

Marichal was working on a shutout in the sixth inning of the third game when he got into a baseline collision with Willie Davis of the Dodgers and Cepeda, our first baseman. Marichal, who injured his right instep on the play, had to be helped off the field. Bob Bolin came in from the bullpen to finish off the 6-0 shutout and save Marichal's 18th win for him. Juan did not pitch again until 17 days later. He did not win another game that season.

In the fourth game against the Dodgers we took a 4-0 lead after three innings. Los Angeles, with my help, came right back to tie the score in the fourth, however. Willie Davis singled to right and when I tried to throw him out as he attempted to stretch it into a double, the ball hit him on the head and he made it all the way to third base. We went in front 5-4 in the eighth only to have Tommy Davis tie the score with a home run in the bottom of the inning. It took a four-run outburst in the ninth for us to finally squelch the Dodgers 9-6. Now we had made some progress. Through the 5th of September the standings looked like this:

	Won	Lost	GB
Los Angeles	91	50	—
San Francisco	89	51	1½

We then returned home for a short five-day stand in Candlestick Park, which turned out to be among the most memorable five days of my career. First we took on the Chicago Cubs and I hit a home run to help Sanford gain the victory. Los Angeles, meanwhile, lost to the Pirates, so that meant that we had whittled the Dodger lead down to just half a game. In our next game I got the most unique stolen base I've ever had. I had moved from first to third on a hit and when I noticed that Ken Hubbs, the Chicago second baseman, took the throw from the outfield and tossed the ball in the air as though he were playing catch by himself, I stole home. We won that game easily, 7-2, but it was a significant day for me because it marked the beginning of a hitting spree that still seems hard for me to believe. I finished that game with hits in my last three times at bat, which in itself, wasn't noteworthy. On the following day I added four more hits, including a double and a game-winning home run, which gave me seven consecutive hits. It also kept us half a game behind the Dodgers and put me within reach of the National League record of 10 straight hits, which dated back to 1897. Half a dozen other players had tied the mark since it had been originally set and now I had a chance to break the record.

Some of my teammates were not too happy with me because I had accepted opportunities to speak at some churches during these few days at home. They felt that I was taxing myself too much by doing added traveling at a time when I should have been sparing my energies for baseball. After going 7 for 7, I went to Palo Alto, some 35 miles from San Franciso, to the Peninsula Bible Church. That night I gave basically the same little talk that I had given in other churches, presenting my Christian testimony and explaining what the Lord meant to me. I didn't know until the service was over that Al Dark was one of the crowd of almost 2,000 people in the audience. He gave me a big smile that night, as if to say that everything was all right.

Lefthander Harvey Haddix was the starting pitcher for the Pirates the next day. I got a single and scored in the first inning. Two innings later I walked. But in the fifth I singled. Now I had nine straight hits. There wasn't a pitcher in the world who was going to get me out on my next trip to the plate, I thought, not because I felt I was the greatest hitter in the game but merely because this was one of those streaks where everything seemed to go right. When I came to bat for the last time that afternoon I had to face ElRoy Face, a relief pitcher. He didn't get me out. On the other hand, I didn't get a hit, since I once again drew a base on balls. We won 4-1 and the Dodgers stayed in front by also winning, but my opportunity to tie or break the record had to wait until the next day.

When I heard that the Pirate pitcher was going to be Tom Sturdivant, a righthanded knuckleballer, I was optimistic about my chances, for I had always done well against him. Not even the ominous presence of a large buzzard hovering over the park before the game could upset me. In the first inning, I came to bat with a runner on first base. Sturdivant's first pitch came in and I slashed it hard on a line between third base and short. As I sped to first base I knew the ball would go through for a hit. Don Hoak, the Pittsburgh third baseman, dived for the ball. He barely got his glove on it but it somehow glanced over to Shortstop Dick Groat, who had moved over to his right. Groat grabbed the ball and threw to second base for a forceout on the runner. I could hardly believe what had taken place. Full credit had to go to Hoak and Groat for a fine defensive play, but I knew that Groat could not have thrown me out at first base. I lost the chance to equal the record because he had been able to get a forceout at second base. As it turned out, that forceout also kept me from tying an all-time major league record of 12 consecutive hits, for in my next two times up I got a single and home run. Los Angeles won that day, too, and as we took off on a 12-day road trip on the night of September 11th the standings read like this:

	Won	Lost	GB
Los Angeles	95	51	—
San Francisco	94	51	½

During my three-day bonanza I had spoken at three churches, once travelling close to 130 miles to Turlock, California. These trips were not an added burden for me and they did not tire me out nearly as much as my teammates thought they would. As far as I could tell, they actually refreshed me and I felt that the Lord gave me the strength to take care of all my obligations both on the field as well as off. On our subsequent road trip I got more rest than I did at home, yet my hitting fell off sharply.

It was a nightmarish trip. Mays, fatigued from the long season, from driving himself game after game and from the tensions of the pennant race, collapsed on the bench during the first game of our trip to Cincinnati. He was taken to the hospital, where his trouble was diagnosed as exhaustion. He was ordered to sit out our next three games. Joey Jay and Jim Maloney of the Reds combined to hold us to four hits in that opening game and beat us 4-1. Jim O'Toole stopped us in the second game of the trip on another four-hitter. When we got to Pittsburgh we were again held to four hits, this time by Earl Francis, who beat us 5-1. Bob Friend of Pittsburgh then defeated us on a five-hitter and the Dodgers moved four games ahead. Our losing streak finally ran to six games but we picked up half a game on Los Angeles when the Dodgers also began to flounder. Nonetheless, things didn't look good for us. We had scored only 12 runs in six games and our pitching staff was feeling the absence of Marichal. I had been of no help whatsoever, getting only one single in 20 times up. Next stop, St. Louis for two games.

We won the first to break our losing streak, but we lost the second. I should say we gave it away, for we made three errors and committed a bases-loaded balk in the ninth inning to lose 5-4. In the hotel lobby before that game, I bumped into Reliefer Ron Perranoski of the Dodgers, who were in town to take the Cardinals on next. I'll never forget his telling me, "You might as well go home to the Dominican Republic. We've got this pennant race all sewed up." After losing to the Cardinals that night we were four games out of first place and I thought that Perranoski might be right. This was no time to give up, however; there were still 10 days left in the season and who could tell what might happen. Two victories in three games in Houston finished our trip on a winning note and when we came back to San Francisco for the final week of play, this was how things looked:

	Won	Lost	GB
Los Angeles	100	56	—
San Francisco	97	59	3

Our position was not good, but when we arrived home I was

encouraged by a talk I had with a close friend named Don Rood. Don, who works for the Pocket Testament League, said, "You've still got a chance. Hundreds, thousands of people in the Bay Area are praying for you and the Giants." I can't say that this gave me any real uplift, but I was beginning to see for the first time just how much support we had. In spite of the disastrous road trip we had just completed, I felt at ease.

After a day off on Monday, September 24th, there remained only six games in which to pick up three lengths on Los Angeles. Because of the slump I had been in and because my elbow was so sore, Dark used Matty in my place in right field against the Cardinals. Matty got two hits and scored twice as we won 4-2. The victory went to Sanford, whose consecutive-game winning streak had ended at 16 on our road trip. A 10-inning home run by Al Spangler of the Colt .45s beat the Dodgers that day and the Los Angeles lead was down two games.

Maury Wills stole his 100th base of the year, Frank Howard drove in five runs and the Dodgers, who had 17 hits, battered Houston 13-1 on Wednesday. We kept pace by winning 6-3 as Billy Pierce gained his 11th victory without a loss at Candlestick Park. Houston came from behind on Thursday to defeat the Dodgers 8-6, but we dropped a 7-4 game to the Cardinals. Then the Cardinals went to Los Angeles and helped us out by edging the Dodgers 3-2 in 10 innings. Our game with Houston was rained out, but we were now within one and a half games of the Dodgers. National League President Warren Giles held a meeting that day to formulate plans for a playoff, should we finish the season tied for first place with the Dodgers. Los Angeles won the flip of the coin and elected to play the opening game of a best-of-three game playoff in San Francisco, with the rest of the action to be held in Chavez Ravine.

Because of the rainout, we had to play a doubleheader with the Colts on Saturday. Cepeda, McCovey and Tom Haller homered for us in the opener and Sanford picked up his 24th victory. Matty, who had two hits in the first game, had two more in the second, including a homer, but Houston Righthander Bob Bruce allowed just four other hits and we lost 4-2. Fortunately for us, the Dodgers were having a hard time getting hits, too, and they lost to the Cardinals 2-0. This meant that we had gained another half game and, with one day to go, we were one length behind Los Angeles. But if we didn't win our final game against Houston, it wouldn't make any difference what the Dodgers did.

O'Dell went after his 20th win for us on that last Sunday. Dick Farrell, a righthander with a good fastball, was on the mound for the

Colt .45s. In Los Angeles, it was Podres of the Dodgers vs. Curt Simmons of the Cardinals. Only four runs were scored by these four teams that afternoon, three of them coming on home runs. Ed Bailey was the first to clear the fence, putting us in front with a fourth-inning homer. Houston tied the score in the sixth and it remained 1-1 until the eighth. Mays led off the inning and hit a curve ball down the right field line that went foul by about 30 feet. He swung at Farrell's next delivery, a high fastball. The ball blurred off Willie's bat, rising on one of the most beautiful flights I've ever seen as it went up and out, clearing the fence in left field and then clattering against the bleacher wall for a home run. It was the 47th homer of the season for Mays. Stu Miller, who had come on to relieve O'Dell in the eighth inning, retired the first two batters in the ninth. Billy Goodman pinch hit for Farrell and when Miller struck him out our hopes, so often on the border of extinction, were still aglow.

We scrambled into the clubhouse and gathered around a radio which was tuned in to the Dodger game. A home run by Gene Oliver gave St. Louis a 1-0 lead in the eighth inning. We waited and listened as patiently as possible. When Curt Simmons got Jim Gilliam of the Dodgers to pop out to second base for the final out in the ninth it wrapped up a 1-0 win for the Cardinals. Pandemonium broke loose in our clubhouse. As I sat on the stool in front of my locker, I thanked God for what He had done for us, enabling us to somehow catch the Dodgers on the final day of the season. Five times during that implausible final week, Matty had come through with two hits in a game. I had started only one game and in that one, I had two hits. There wasn't much time to reminisce; we had to get ready to take on the Dodgers the next day in the first game of the playoff series. Somebody asked Dark if he thought we would be at a disadvantage if the series went the three-game limit because we would have to play the last two days in Chavez Ravine. "I don't care where they are played, here or in Lake Charles, Louisiana," Dark replied. Both of us had come a long way from Lake Charles and I could only wonder how much further we would go in the next few days.

CHAPTER *12*

MUCH TO BE THANKFUL FOR

Everybody on both sides was weary even before the playoffs started. The Dodgers had had only three complete games during the frantic last month and that had placed a heavy burden on the bullpen, with Perranoski being called on 14 times, Roebuck 12 and Sherry nine. L.A. had a 13-14 record in September and had lost 10 of its last 13 games. Part of the downfall stemmed from a flurry of errors, 38 of them in those final 27 contests. Our pitching staff was also over-worked and had had only eight complete games in September, four each by O'Dell and Sanford. The two most dependable relief pitchers were Don Larsen, who was used nine times, and Stu Miller, who worked in 11 games and who pitched eight innings during the last two days.

Dodger Manager Walt Alston decided to start Koufax in the opening game. Koufax had started only twice since he had been disabled with circulatory trouble in his pitching hand two months earlier. In his first try he lasted two-thirds of an inning. The next time out he went five innings. He had also been used in a brief relief job once. The consensus of opinion was that Koufax was far from being the overpowering pitcher he had once been. Pierce was scheduled to go for us and had two things in his favor: he was well-rested and he still hadn't lost in Candlestick Park. He got the first three batters he faced in that game to pop up to the infield. With two out in the bottom of the inning, I lined a pitch from Koufax into the left field corner for a double. Mays followed with a home run to right-center. After Koufax had given up a home run to Jim Davenport and a single to Ed Bailey in the second inning, Alston sent Leo Durocher, one of his coaches, to the mound to tell Sandy what he already knew.

Mays and Cepeda hit back-to-back homers in the sixth, for Willie his 49th, for Orlando his 35th. In the eighth inning, the Dodger raggedness really showed as we increased our lead to 8-0. First, the Dodger pitchers gave up three bases on balls. Then Jose Pagan doubled to right field to score two runners. The last run came in when Frank Howard's throw from right field hit Maury Wills in the head. Pierce finished up with a three-hit shutout and we were off to Los Angeles for the second game of the playoffs.

That game was a perfect example of the unpredictability of base-ball. I doubled again my first time up, this time driving in Cepeda in the second inning with the first run of the game. We routed Dodger starter Don Drysdale with four runs in the sixth and were sitting on a comfortable 5-0 lead. All we had to do was hang on for another four innings and the pennant would be ours. When Sanford walked the Dodger leadoff man in the sixth, Dark took him out and brought in Miller. Suddenly, it was a new ball game. The Dodgers, who hadn't scored for 35 innings, broke loose for seven runs. We scored twice in the eighth to tie the score at 7-7, but in the ninth the Dodgers got three walks and finally, after a record four hours and 18 minutes, a sacrifice fly that gave them an improbable 8-7 victory. The most improbable game was yet to come, however.

Before that decisive game of the playoffs, Dark said to me, "I think we'd better pray about this one." I told him, "I don't think we'll have to pray any more. I prayed last night and this morning and I know that God will give us the victory." Dark smiled a bit.

We took an early lead, scoring twice in the third inning off Dodger Lefthander Johnny Podres. Marichal was pitching for us but he wasn't sharp. This was his third start since being hurt four weeks earlier and for the third time in a row he was driven from the mound. He surrendered a run in the fourth and lost the lead in the sixth when Tommy Davis hit a two-run homer. Wills stole his 103rd and 104th bases of the season in the seventh, then scored on an error to put the Dodgers in front 4-2.

Ed Roebuck, who had relieved Podres in the sixth, kept us from scoring and as we went into the ninth inning we still were trailing by two runs. As I came in from the outfield at the end of the eighth inning, I vividly recall saying to myself, "God, I know that you can help us win this game." Instead of sitting on the bench and waiting for my turn to hit, I went into the clubhouse to listen to the game on radio. Matty was sent up to lead off the ninth inning as a pinch hitter for Reliefer Don Larsen and he singled. Harvey Kuenn then hit into a forceout, a play on which he really hustled and got to first base before he could be doubled up. We had only two outs left now and if we didn't score two runs the season would be over for us.

It was almost time for me to bat, so I headed for the dugout. My heart should have been thumping, but it wasn't and I am sure it was because I had put my reliance on God instead of on myself. Willie McCovey, pinch hitting for Chuck Hiller, drew a walk, putting runners on first and second. Roebuck then walked me on a 3-2 pitch and now we had the bases loaded. Mays wasted no time and banged the first pitch off Roebuck's bare hand. As the ball squirted away from

Roebuck, Mays made it to first and the rest of us moved up a base, with Kuenn crossing home plate. That made the score 4-3. Roebuck, pitching for the sixth time in seven days, was obviously tiring, so Alston brought in Stan Williams to try to stop us.

Cepeda hit the second pitch from Williams to right field, deep enough to bring in the tying run and to allow me to move to base after the catch. Mays went from first to second on a wild pitch that didn't roll far enough away to let me score. Ed Bailey, the batter at the time, was intentionally walked, loading the bases. Jim Davenport then worked the count to three balls and one strike. Williams' next pitch was ball four and that forced me across with the lead run. When Dodger Second Baseman Larry Burright made an error on Jose Pagan's ground ball, Mays scored to give us a 6-4 lead. Bob Nieman pinch hit for Matty and went down swinging for the third out, but we went into the bottom of the ninth with a two-run lead. Now it was the Dodgers who were within three outs of being eliminated.

Dark brought in Billy Pierce to face the Dodgers and he got Wills to ground out to third base and Gilliam to fly out to center. Lee Walls came up to hit for Burright and on the third pitch flied out to Mays in center field. We had won! The pennant was ours!

Minutes later the scene in our clubhouse was one of delirious joy. Emotions, pent up for months, unravelled themselves in spontaneous outbursts. The pennant we had almost dared not to think about now belonged to us. Somebody poured beer or champagne over my head as I was dragged in front of a television camera to say a few words. As soon as I got through with that I elbowed my way over to my locker, shook hands with a few teammates and enjoyed the excitement of the hour. There was one thing I had not done yet, however, and I knew it. Our clubhouse was a cacophony of noise, but over to my right I saw a quiet spot; it was the shower room and it was there that I went to bow down and thank God for the victory He had granted us.

In a room to the left, Dark was besieged by newsmen. Someone offered Dark a paper cup filled with champagne but he declined, saying, "I don't need any help to be happy at a time like this." He also said something else that made me proud. He told the writers, "I'm sorry for what happened to Koufax this year. His injury made the difference and gave us a chance."

Dark had done a lot for us in our fight for the pennant. He had said something in spring training that I believe made an impression on a number of us. "The hardest thing to teach a player," Dark had said some seven months earlier, "is that winning is more important than going 4 for 4 at bat yourself. The saddest thing to me is to hear a player whose team has lost, whistling in the clubhouse because he had a good day at the plate." Al knew he wasn't saying something new to us, but he got his message across. Dark had taught us to play as a team, not as individuals and now he was able to enjoy the fruits of his teaching.

He had also instilled in us the extra effort needed to take advantage of even the smallest breaks. Alvin had fought for us, cajoled us, scolded us, encouraged us and had never let us give up. We won the pennant with what was regarded as a so-so pitching staff, a staff that was crippled by injuries. It was in the handling of the pitchers that Dark may have exercised his talents best of all. He was expert at knowing when to take out a starter and bring in a reliefer, a move that seems simple on the surface but which is actually a delicate art. It is hard to appreciate just how difficult it is for a manager to walk out to the mound and tell a pitcher who has a record of, let's say 16-4, that he is through and that he is to be replaced by a pitcher with a 3-4 record. That pitcher with a 16-4 won-lost record is a big winner and he expects to be treated like one. But Dark was never afraid of what a star pitcher might say or think; he did what he felt was right. He approached the game much as a general approaches a battle, making the decisions and accepting full responsibility for them.

In my heart I was happy, yet I couldn't stop thinking about the Dodgers. I will always carry in my mind a picture of the Dodgers, heads bowed, faces sad, some with tears in their eyes, as they walked slowly to their clubhouse after that final playoff game. They had battled us right down to the last inning of the last game and their defeat must have been painful. The final standings told only that we had won, but could never convey the ecstasy that we knew or the haunting despair that engulfed the Dodgers. Here is how the pennant race wound up:

	Won	Lost	GB
San Francisco	103	62	—
Los Angeles	102	63	1

Now that the pennant was ours, we had to take on the New York Yankees, the American League champions, in the World Series. We did not have the luxury of a day off to relax and get ready, for the playoffs had already postponed the start of the Series one day. The Yankees, anticipating our victory after we had won the first game of the playoffs, had already flown to San Francisco. Our flight from Los Angeles back home was a pleasant one. All went well until we were getting ready to come in for a landing. Then we learned that there were some 50,000 people mobbing the airport and spilling onto the airfield. Our pilot had to circle for an hour and 20 minutes and when he finally brought us down he took us to a maintenance depot about a mile from where we were to have landed. Not even this maneuver could free us of the fans, who came swarming over to the area to shout their congratulations. A few of them got out of hand and smashed several of the windows on the bus that was to take us into town.

Whitey Ford, the redoubtable lefthander, was the Yankee pitcher in the opening game of the World Series. Billy O'Dell was our pitcher. He had won 19 games during the regular season, two more than Whitey, but he got into deep trouble in the very first inning. After striking out Tony Kubek to start the game, O'Dell gave up singles to Bobby Richardson and Tom Tresh. Mickey Mantle worked the count to 3 and 2 and then went down swinging. Up came Roger Maris, who in the past three seasons had hit 133 home runs, including a record 61 the year before. He hit a long drive to deep right field. I took off after the ball, leaped as high as I could and, as I crashed full force into the fence, got my glove on the ball. My glove was well above the 10-foot wire fence and as I came down my arm banged against the top of it and the ball was jarred loose. I had deprived Maris of a home run, but he got a double when the ball fell to the ground in front of me. Two Yankee runners scored.

Ford put us down one-two-three in the bottom of the first, getting me for the final out on a dribbler down the first-base line. In the second inning, though, Mays singled, went to third on another single by Davenport and then scored on a surprise bunt by Pagan. It was the first run off Ford after a record 33 2/3 scoreless innings of World Series competition. Tresh opened the Yankee third with a line drive to short right-center on which I made a diving catch. The Yankees didn't score that inning but we did, to tie the game up. Chuck Hiller led off with a double and I sent him to third with a single to left. Mays then drove Hiller in with another single. There was no more scoring until the seventh inning when Clete Boyer put the Yankees ahead with a home run. New York added two more runs in the eighth and another in the ninth to beat us 6-2.

Each team had its winningest pitcher ready for the second game; Ralph Terry, 23-12, was the Yankee starter; Jack Sanford, 24-7, was going for us. Hiller hit Terry's first pitch of the afternoon on a line into the right-field corner, where Maris almost made a sensational catch. The ball got away from Maris and Hiller was credited with a double. I bunted the first pitch to me down the first-base side, sacrificing Hiller to third on the play. Hiller then scored when Matty bounced out to second base. McCovey added another run in the seventh on a 425-foot homer. Sanford, although hampered by a bad cold, limited the Yankees to just three hits and shut them out 2-0 to even the Series at one victory apiece. I'll never forget McCovey's reply when a writer asked him if he had ever hit a longer homer. Said Willie in a typical burst of verbosity, "Yep."

After that game we flew to New York, where, following a day off, we resumed play at Yankee Stadium. Before the game, Dark informed me that he was switching me from right field, where I had played all year, to left. His reason, he explained, was that left field was the most difficult spot to play in Yankee Stadium. (It is right field, with its glaring sun and the most unpredictable winds in all of baseball, that is the toughest outfield position to play in Candlestick Park.) I accepted the assignment as merely another challenge in a year that had already been crammed full of adventures.

I didn't have to wait long to see if I would be able to handle the job in left field, for in the first four innings three hard line drives came whizzing my way. Tony Kubek hit the third pitch from Billy Pierce to left and I pocketed it without any trouble. My most difficult chance came in the next inning when Elston Howard connected solidly and drove the ball almost to the left field wall, where I made a one-hand grab after a long run. After I caught Mantle's liner in the fourth inning I didn't have another fly ball hit to me all afternoon.

Pierce, meanwhile, was in a scoreless pitching duel with Bill Stafford of the Yankees. It wasn't until the seventh inning that New York scored. Tresh opened with a single and then Mantle hit the ball sharply to left for another single. Mantle's ball took a wicked high hop and got past me, allowing Tresh to advance to third base and Mantle to second. I was charged with an error on the play. McCovey, playing in right field, was given an error on the next ball, a hard liner by Maris that went for a single before Willie booted the ball away and gave him an extra base. The Yankees had a 2-0 lead and were soon to make it 3-0. Maris took third on a long fly and then, after Moose Skowron had been hit by a pitch, scored when we barely missed pulling off an inning-ending double play because the ball got stuck momentarily in the webbing of Second Baseman Chuck Hiller's glove.

There was a man on first base when I came to bat in the eighth and when I saw my line drive hit Stafford on the left shin it looked as though we might have a good rally going. Stafford, however, chased the ball down and threw me out at first on a play I have to give him a lot of credit for. It was only after he got me out that he fell to the ground in pain. After a few minutes of rest and a few whiffs of smelling salts he got the third out of the inning. He had allowed only two hits until the ninth, then gave up a double to Mays and a two-out home run to Bailey. That was it, though, and the Yankees clung to a 3-2 win.

In game No. 4 I was put into the cleanup spot, making it the fourth different spot I had been used in during the Series. Dark had me hitting third in the opener, No. 2 in the second game and leadoff in the third contest. I led off the second inning by hitting Whitey Ford's first pitch just inside the third-base line for a double. Two outs later, Tom Haller hit a 3-2 pitch into the left field seats to give us a 2-0 lead. Marichal was pitching for us and had shut out the Yankees on two hits over the first four innings. In the fifth inning, however, Juan was injured when the ball hit his right hand as he tried to bunt.

Fastballer Bob Bolin, who came on in relief for us, gave up two hits in the fifth and got away with it. Then he gave up two hits in the sixth and did *not* get away with it. The Yankees, who had tied the score, had pinch hit for Ford and now they had to bring in a relief pitcher. After Matty got a pinch double to put runners on second and third with one out, Marshall Bridges came in to pitch for the Yankees. Bridges intentionally walked pinch-hitter Bob Nieman, loading the bases. Kuenn struck out and Hiller came up. He homered. It was the first grand slam homer ever hit by a National Leaguer in World Series competition and it led us to a 7-3 win. The Series was now tied at two victories for each club.

Rain postponed the fifth game one day. Although we outhit the Yankees eight to six (I had a triple and single), Ralph Terry was tough on us in the clutch and beat us 5-3. The most damaging Yankee hit was a three-run homer by Tresh with the score 2-2 in the eighth. So, we all had to go back to the West Coast to wrap up the Series and, with the Yankees leading 3-2 in games played, we were in a bad position.

Then came the downpour. I have never seen so much rain. It seemed as if the cascade of water came from an overhead waterfall rather than from rain clouds. The sixth game was postponed one day, then another.

We shared a two-family house with Marichal and his wife that year and when Juan and I weren't talking baseball or looking out at the wind and rain, we listened to my short-wave radio. About the only thing I left the house for was to take my family to the airport because they had to get home to the Dominican Republic. When I returned from the airport, I went to bed. A few hours later, at about 2 in the morning, the phone rang. Foggily, I reached for the phone. It was my friend Don Rood. I wasn't enthusiastic about being awakened at that hour, even if it was Don. What he had to say, though, brought me awake sharply, for it was some of the best news ever. Jose Pagan, my friend, teammate and roommate for several years now, had accepted Christ that night, Rood told me. After hanging up the phone, I thought about Jose, about how we had read the Bible together—the one given me by Roque Martinez—and about how we had talked in uncertain terms about what it might mean. Jose—as I curled up in bed I could see him, and if there wasn't a smile on my lips as I drifted back to sleep, there was certainly one on my heart. The first time I saw Jose after that was in the clubhouse the next day. He was waiting in front of my locker, bubbling with conversation about how happy he felt about letting Jesus Christ into his heart.

After the World Series had been postponed for two days, both teams journeyed some 90 miles to hold workouts in Modesto, where, almost miraculously, the rain had passed by. Finally, after three post-ponements, the sixth game was played on October 15th. It was Ford against Pierce in a duel of lefthanders. With one away in the fourth inning of a scoreless game, I singled and went to second when Mays walked. Ford then whirled around to try to pick me off second base. His throw was bad, bouncing into right field and coming to a rest on the soggy turf. I scored on the play and Mays made it to third base. A double by Cepeda and a single by Davenport gave us a 3-0 lead. In the fifth inning I had one of our four singles as we built up a 5-0 advantage. Pierce, meanwhile, retired the first 13 Yankees before Maris homered in the fifth. He allowed only two more hits and wound up a 5-2 winner.

Thus, the World Series came down to the seventh and final game, with Terry going for the Yankees and Sanford for us. It was a superb pitching performance by both. New York scored in the fifth inning as we completed a double play. There are some who contend that Dark erred when he ordered the infield to play back for the double play, arguing that he conceded one run. Well, it's hard to say. Ours had been a hard-hitting team all year, one that scored often, and giving up one run that early in the game didn't seem disastrous at the time. Had we gone for the one out at home plate instead, the Yankees would have been able to send one more batter to the plate in that inning; that extra man would have been Tresh, who led the team in hitting during the Series.

In the ninth inning we had an excellent chance to tie or win the game. Matty came in to pinch hit and beat out a drag bunt to open the inning. I bunted the first pitch foul, fouled off the second and then went down swinging. There were just two outs left to us and after Hiller struck out (he also tried unsuccessfully to bunt once) it was up to Mays. He doubled to right field and only fine fielding by Maris kept Matty from scoring. Ralph Houk came out to the mound to talk over the situation with Terry, who decided he would rather pitch to McCovey than to walk him and have to face Cepeda. In his previous at bat, McCovey had tripled and only a sensational catch by Tresh in left field, which had robbed Mays of a hit, had kept us from scoring. This time, McCovey hit a ball deep to right field, but it curved foul. He hit the next ball hard, too, but Second Baseman Bobby Richardson made a leaping one-hand catch for the out that made the Yankees the World Champions.

We had come so very close to winning—as close as the 1-0 score of that final game indicated. It was the sort of Series that caused you to replay certain situations over and over again. Suppose the double play ball had not become stuck in Hiller's glove in the third game? Suppose Hiller or I had been able to bunt Matty to second base in the ninth inning of the seventh game so that he could have scored on the double by Mays? Suppose—it could go on and on, and the Yankees, had they lost, could have come up with just as many supposes. We had lost, and that was it.

As for myself, I had tied for the club lead in Series hits with seven, although my .269 batting average was far behind the .368 that Pagan had to top all hitters on both teams. During the playoffs I had hit .333. And my regular-season average of .316 had placed me seventh in the league. On top of that, I had career highs of 25 home runs and 98 runs batted in. I felt that I had overcome the "jammer" quite successfully.

Before Alvin Dark took over as manager of our Giants, there had been all sorts of stories about racial trouble on the club. There was talk that the whites and the Negroes were ready to come to blows and that the situation was equally bad between the whites and Latins and the Negroes and Latins. I may have been a little naive, but I was never aware that there was any racial tension in our clubhouse. Oh sure, there were cliques. Most of the Latins stuck together, a camaraderie that was inspired more by a similarity in language and habit than anything else. Most Negroes stuck together. Most whites stuck together. None of us saw anything wrong with this. It was not a caste system; we all had equal rights to do as we wished.

Dark had a very simple and effective idea. He broke up the arrangement of lockers in our clubhouse, seeing to it that there was more of an intermingling between races. No longer were all the Negroes grouped in one corner of the clubhouse, all the whites and Latins in other corners. This forced us to get to know each other better, for we were now seated next to players other than those we hung around with after the game. It gave us a better understanding of each other because the more we chatted together the more we found out about each other's family, hopes, aches, bills and beliefs.

Baseball has done a remarkable job of bringing about an equality.

Much To Be Thankful For

I have been coming to the United States for 11 years to play baseball and I can truthfully say that if it were not for the rioting which occasionally occurs I would not be aware of any race problem. As far as I'm concerned, it is almost nonexistent in baseball. There will always remain, I suppose, a certain amount of intolerance. Latins generally come from countries where they are in the majority and where there are no race problems. They don't grow up, as American Negroes have had to in many instances, with a feeling of inferiority or with a feeling of rebellion against the white man. When Latins come to America to play baseball they are often shocked by the racial issue and by its scope. On the other hand, the American Negroes are cognizant of racial differences throughout their lives and when they get to the major leagues they don't suddenly stop being alert to it. For the Negro the situation is ever present. For the Latin it is far away.

I respect the effort of the honest and sincere Negro to stand up for his rights, to express his feelings, to give of his time to help his people and, if necessary, to give his life. My respect, however, is held for those who act with discretion and whose lives and passions are ruled by common sense and a stability of mind and action. Those who find it imperative to turn to violence to support their views are, in my mind, doing more harm than good.

Certainly, the white man has been guilty of many crimes against the Negro, but how can flag-waving Negroes who are fighting for equality suddenly consider it proper to trample on the rights of others by destroying businesses and homes, by carrying on hysterically and violently, by using guns and throwing Molotov cocktails? I am reasonably certain that a good deal of this behavior is incited by communist agitators. This means that Negro rioters, upset because they feel their lives are being dominated and manipulated by white men, are actually having their lives manipulated by communists.

You may scoff at me and say that I am overstating the case. I can only reply by saying that I have had dealings with communists and have seen how cleverly they work. People talk about my homeland and say how terrible it is that we have so many riots and killings there. I agree with them. What I don't understand, though, is how some of these people (both white and Negro) who are so distressed about the inhumanity of man to man in other parts of the world can be so callous, so downright cruel and inhuman toward their fellow countrymen.

I am proud to be a ballplayer in America. I can see so clearly how much better the race relations are inside the game than outside. Just imagine for a few moments what it would be like if ballplayers decided to use some of the tactics used in racial clashes in other parts of the nation. What would the reaction be if a group of hooded Negro players rode up to Mickey Mantle's home and threw a hand grenade through his living room window? How would Americans feel if Willie Mays were severely beaten up a group of white players? Exactly how to create a brotherhood among men is hard to say, but the Bible does offer much advice, including the golden rule of Luke 6: 31 (KJV): "And as ye would that men should do to you, do ye also to them likewise."

I have had a few white people come to me and, in a very sincere way, let me know that they felt sorry for me because my complexion is tan. It seems to me that the white man's thinking is not entirely clear on the value he places on skin coloration. To him, my tan complexion and all that it stands for is less than desirable, yet he spends millions of dollars and millions of hours in his worshipful pursuit of the sun and a similar tan. And when he achieves that coloration he feels more manly and feels that he has attained a status symbol that tells the world where he has been. At least my color is God given and won't peel off or fade away. I agree with the white man who has a tan; it looks nice.

There was no chance to play any winter ball during the off-season because my country was in a political upheaval. While I was at home I did little thinking about baseball, choosing instead to do some thanking. I couldn't stop thanking the Lord for having helped me and for having helped our team. Above all, I was grateful for Jose's salvation. I could only wonder how important the rain had been in that situation. Had we been able to play our final World Series games on schedule, it is likely that Jose would have already been on his way home to Puerto Rico on the day that turned out to be his day of acceptance of Jesus Christ. I thought about Don Rood and what he had told me about the prayers of all those faithful people. There were so many unanswerables. Would Jose have come to Christ when he did had we not tied for the pennant, gone through the playoffs and entered the Series? I don't presume to know how the Lord works. My satisfaction came from knowing that He works out all things according to His will.

I invited Jose to come to my home during the winter and I recall that he arrived on a Friday and that while he was with me he attended services at the church I belong to, the Templo Biblico in Santo Domingo. That night he gave his first public testimony concerning his acceptance of Christ. I was so happy I almost cried. We also went fishing. On one trip we caught 300 pounds of fish and I got an enormous lobster that weighed close to 13 pounds.

Although disappointed that I couldn't play winter ball, I found that there was more time for other things, more time to plunge into a study of the Bible, more time with my family, more time to relax. Quite often I went up to the northern coast to talk to people, to show them the Bible, to try to help them with their problems. The more closely I worked with them the more I saw their need, the wretchedness of their lives, the little hope that any of them had. Best of all, I had the privilege of seeing some of these people understand the Bible and accept Jesus Christ.

I felt that the Lord had been so good, so kind to me that I wanted to do something for Him and when the chance came to go to Venezuela to work there with the Pocket Testament League, I went gladly. They were the 8 most thrilling days of my life.

We gave out thousands of copies of the Gospel of John to the people in Venezuela and I also had the opportunity to tell them of the joy I had personally known since coming to Christ Jesus. We worked long hours and did a lot of travelling and yet I never once felt weary. Our journeys carried us to Caracas, Barcelona, a small country jail, an air force base, and wherever we went I was excited to find that people were willing to listen to me. I think they were let down at first when they found I had not come to give them tips on how to hit and field and run and yet they were attentive to what I had to say about my Christian beliefs. This was true even in the smallest hamlets, where, I am sure, there were many people who didn't know who I was and even if they did, couldn't have cared less. Our group stayed in the homes of missionaries of all denominations in these towns and when it was time to go back home I felt greatly blessed because I had met so many fine people, and by this I mean both Christians and non-Christians. People — eager, sincere, searching people — were to be found anywhere, be it San Francisco, Haina or Caracas. I could see that there was much work to be done.

It is important to me that I can work with people of all denominations. In my own country there is opportunity to witness with Baptists, Methodist, and just about every other Protestant group.

My theory concerning the miniature type of ministry I had taken up was that I wanted to tell people about the best thing that had ever happened to me, about how life now had a purpose other than just trying to be a good ballplayer. It's strange, I thought, that men so often try to keep their riches to themselves. A gold miner, having found a treasure, is unlikely to tell others, fearing they will take from him what he feels is his. Christians, I found, were the opposite, gladly telling others of how they had found Christ Jesus and how they could come to know Him too. Throughout 1962 and the winter of 1963 I had seen so many examples of the Lord working in my life. I had the pleasure of knowing that Jose Pagan had made his decision for Christ and that others had done likewise. And, with the Lord's help, I had become a much better ballplayer. Ever since then I have told myself that when in doubt, I should never limit God, who can do so much and who gives us the strength to do that which we could never accomplish on our own.

CHAPTER 13

HERE COME THE LATINS

One of the most gratifying aspects of my career is that I have been part of the wave of Latins coming up to the major leagues. People back home regard me as the first Dominican to reach the majors. They tell me that Ozzie Virgil, who was a Giant two years before me, doesn't count because he left the Dominican Republic at a very young age and by the time he got to the majors he was an American citizen. Although Latins are now an integral part of baseball, this has not always been so. As late as 1948, there was just one Latin in the majors. There were five the following season and slightly more than two dozen in 1959. Year by year the number has risen and in 1966 there were 64 Latins on the spring training rosters. Not all of those players made their teams, but others who were not on the rosters, such as Pitcher Minnie Rojas of the California Angels, came up later in the season.

Exactly who was the first Latin in the big leagues is not clear. There is some evidence that Estaban Enrique Bellan, an infielder with the Troy Haymakers of the original National Association, was the first. His nickname was Steve, but his birthplace is believed to have been Cuba. If Bellan was not the first, then the honor would go to Vincent Nava, who was born in San Francisco but whose real name was Irwin Sandy and whose parents were Mexican. He broke in with Providence of the National League in 1882 and was the first major leaguer to become the target of racial abuse.

This epic of how the Latin has become an accepted part of the game had its real genesis in 1911. It is appropriate that the English language, which gives so many of us so much trouble, was so important in bringing the Latin into baseball. In fact, the two players who began the Latin influx would not have achieved this had not one of them been able to speak English.

It was back in 1911 that Charles Bancroft, secretary of the Cincinnati Reds, returned from a vacation in Cuba and could hardly wait to tell the people back home what he had seen. Unlike the typical tourist, Bancroft was not anxious to spew out details about the beauty of the Gulf of Mexico, the Morro Castle or the vast tobacco plantations. What Bancroft wanted to talk about was a ballplayer, a Cuban ballplayer named Rafael Almeida. Here, raved Bancroft, was a third baseman who couldn't field like Pie Traynor—yet—and a batter who couldn't hit like Ty Cobb—yet. But give him time, Bancroft begged Cincinnati Manager Clark Griffith, just give him a chance and the Reds would never be sorry.

Griffith listened to Bancroft's carryings on and yawned indifferently. Havana, in those less enlightened days, was much further from Cincinnati than it is today. All that Griffith could picture was some nincompoop running around, swinging a banana stalk for a bat and wearing a banana peel for a glove. Bancroft was insistent, however. He refused to let Griffith pass up this bargain and he saw to it that a cable was dispatched to Havana for Rafael Almeida, offering him a tryout with the Reds in the spring of 1911.

Back came a cable from Almeida:

WILL REPORT FOR TRYOUT IF YOU PAY ALSO
EXPENSES MY INTERPRETER.   GRACIAS.

When Griffith read that, he decided right then and there never to have anything to do with another Latin ballplayer. Bancroft kept plugging away, though, and another cable was sent to Almeida, this time inviting both the third baseman and his interpreter to come ahead.

By the time that Almeida made his appearance at the Cincinnati training camp that spring, even Griffith was getting anxious to have a look at this prodigy. Almeida and his interpreter both suited up for the opening workout. After a while, Bancroft nervously sidled up to Griffith to ask if he was going to sign Almeida to a contract with the Reds.

"I'm going to sign up a young Cuban," said Griffith, "but not the one you've been telling me about for months. The one I'm interested in is the interpreter. The other one can't carry his glove."

Actually, the Reds signed both Marsans, the interpreter, and Almeida. As things turned out, Griffith proved to be a better judge of talent than Bancroft. Both Almeida and Marsans played in their first major league game on July 4th, 1911 in the morning half of a doubleheader in Chicago. Although Almeida batted .313 in 26 games that first season and Marsans .261 in 36 games, it was the interpreter who prevailed in the years that followed. Marsans batted .317 in 110 games in 1912, hit .297 the next season and lasted almost eight years in the big leagues. Almeida was through after three seasons. More important than the statistics was the fact that the breakthrough had been made and that Latins had gained entry into the major leagues.

Down through the years the majority of Latins who have come to

America to play professional ball have, like Almeida, not been on good terms with the English language. Unlike Almeida, few have had the luxury of interpreters. Occasionally, a fringe Latin player was retained by a club to serve as an interpreter so that there would be some semblance of communication between a manager and his pupils. Language problems are not solved easily.

When Paul Richards was the manager of the Chicago White Sox in the early 1950s, he became irritated by all the jabbering going on among the Latin ballplayers in his clubhouse. Richards called his players to attention one day and told them firmly, "The only language I want spoken around here is Chicago White Sox."

One of the members of the White Sox in those days was Minnie Minoso, a blithe spirit if ever there was one. Minnie was always a lively, talkative person who, alas, found it impossible to refrain from speaking his native Spanish. In his own inimitable fashon, however, Minnie found a way around his predicament, a way which melted the stern Paul Richards and even caused him to fracture his face with an occasional smile. Whenever Minoso caught himself rattling off Spanish within earshot of Richards he would always make certain that he concluded his conversation by saying, "Chicago White Sox."

Connie Marrero, who was a pitcher with the Washington Senators during that same period, was another Cuban with a winning way. There are some who insist that he was close to the age of 50 before he joined the Senators in 1950. Whatever his age, Marrero made it known quickly that he did not understand a word of English and that he hadn't the faintest idea of how to utter a word of this strange language. It was a convenient ploy, but one day he gave himself away. This came about in one of his early games after he had struck out Ted Williams of the Boston Red Sox with the bases loaded. As soon as the exuberant Marrero got back to the dugout after that feat he said loud and clear, "Good pitch. More money." It was in 1964 that Birdie Tebbetts, then manager of the Cleveland Indians, shelled out $700 for a course in how to speak Spanish.

While he was managing the Senators a few years ago, Cookie Lavagetto decided that it might be wise to learn a little Spanish so that he could communicate more freely with his Latin players. Lavagetto had intended to sign up for a home-study course, then decided it would be simpler and more effective to go right to one of his players for firsthand lessons. He asked one of his Latins to teach him a few key phrases so that he could parcel out instructions to base runners. Lavagetto first asked how to instruct a runner to break up a double play and when the Latin player gave him the magic words, Cookie went home and recited them over and over again. The first time the team had a Latin runner on first base, Cookie, eager to exploit his newfound talent as a linguist, made certain that he passed along his advice to him in Spanish. Jose Valdivielso, a Cuban, was the runner. After listening to what his manager had to say, Jose looked at Cookie and then, raising his eyebrows, nodded that he understood.

When the next batter hit a ground ball, Valdivielso did not hustle down to second base and did not even bother to slide in an attempt to break up the double play. Lavagetto was in a rage. He went to Julio Becquer, another of his Cuban ballplayers, and asked him for the meaning of the Spanish words which he had been taught. Replied Becquer, "That means to, 'Walk nicely to the man on second base.' "

Cookie took the whole affair in good stride, realizing, as he put it, that, "A Cuban is a pleasant fellow. If he understands you, he nods his head, smiles and says, 'Si, si.' If he doesn't understand you, he nods his head, smiles and says, 'Si, si.' "

A few years earlier, the late Charlie Dressen, then the manager of the Senators, also had trouble with Latin baserunners. He decided one day that he needed a pinch runner and motioned to Pedro Ramos, a Cuban pitcher with fast feet, to replace the runner on first base. Ramos sped from first to third on a single. Dressen, not wanting to take a chance on any misunderstanding that might cost his side a valuable run, called time so that he could talk over the situation with Ramos. Charlie began talking, going over the various things he wanted his runner to be aware of. Then, in mid-sentence, Dressen's mouth hung wide open; he had finally noticed that Ramos had been shrugging his shoulders to indicate that he didn't comprehend a word of the priceless advice being given him. Dressen waved Ramos out of the game and brought in another runner to take over at third base, an American who could understand what Charlie had to say. Thus, because of the language problem, Dressen had been forced into one of the most unique bits of strategy of his career, using a pinch runner for a pinch runner.

Dressen also had difficulties with another Cuban, Outfielder Carlos Paula, whose ability to hit the ball hard and often was exceeded only by his ability to invent stories about why he had to hurry back home to Havana for a few days. At last count, Paula was known to have had six grandmothers who passed away in Havana.

Paula had a knack for making even the most outlandish of his excuses sound plausible. One spring he showed up at the Washington training camp in Orlando, Florida and almost immediately began making it known that he would have to make a quick trip to Tampa to pick up some of his clothes. He was granted permission to go to Tampa. A week went by and Paula had not returned to camp. Dressen was genuinely worried and wanted to have the Federal Bureau of Investigation called in to start a search for his missing outfielder. At last, after an absence of about 10 days, Paula arrived back in Orlando. By this time, Dressen had heard reliable rumors that Paula had ventured to Havana during his absence. When Dressen encountered Paula on his first day back in uniform he asked him, "How do you get to Tampa by way of Havana?"

"I lose my way," Paula explained, a mischievous grin flickering across his face.

Dressen, an understanding man, replied, "I guess they just don't mark the highways the way they used to."

Many of us have encountered the loneliness that Paula must have faced. To experience loneliness is one thing; to know it—to begin to struggle with it, to try to understand it—is something deeper. There is a unique power to the aloneness that comes from not being able to communicate. It is always possible to use sign language to establish a rudimentary acquaintance, to exploit the few words one *does* know, but when these shallow wells of contact are evaporated there remains only the uneasy, helpless shrug, the look of futility, the nod, wave or handshake of goodbye.

Not knowing the English language when you are playing in the United States is a drawback that can have calamitous culinary repercussions. There was one Latin player who, because he couldn't speak much English, kept ordering the one thing he did know how to ask for—hamburgers—for breakfast, lunch and dinner. Other Latins have had similar problems. One of them learned how to pronounce the names of two new dishes in English and the next morning went to a restaurant and confidently ordered both. A few minutes later the waitress dutifully returned with two plates, one containing an order of scrambled eggs, the other piled with spaghetti. Another Latin sat down for dinner one night and mistakenly ate an entire bowl of gravy, thinking it was some kind of soup. It is fortunate that, sooner or later, some thoughtful teammate always takes notice of these hungry souls before they waste away.

My English is fairly good now, but not long ago I learned that if you throw a hanging, or not-too-clear, order at a waitress she will hit it right out of the dining room. This latest incident took place at the Roosevelt Hotel, which is where the Braves stay when in New York City to play the Mets. The waitress had asked for my breakfast order and I had told her that I wanted two four- or five-minute eggs. She said a little testily, "Well, make up your mind." I replied, "Okay, make it five." When she came back with my order she brought me a large bowl with five eggs.

Not being able to speak precise English can be a curse. Being able to speak Spanish, however, can be a blessing. When Shortstop Julio Gotay, a Puerto Rican, teamed up with Second Baseman Julian Javier, a Dominican, for the St. Louis Cardinals a few years ago they were able to have strategy conferences right on the field in front of opposing runners.

And then there was Adolfo Luque, the gifted righthander from Havana. He didn't win a game in the majors until he was 28 years old, but then went on to win another 193 before he turned 45. There was a great deal of wisdom, as well as mispronunciation, in the way Luque referred to two of his favorite pitches as his "change of space" and his "coy ball."

One of the things that made it so difficult for Latins to pick up the English language is that so many of us return to our home country after the baseball season is over, there to speak nary a word of English until it is time to return to the United States the following year for spring training. There is no doubt that the best way to learn English is to engage in as many conversations as possible with those who already speak it well. Reading American newspapers and magazines and listening to radio and television also are helpful. Some players have gone so far as to go to American movies and watch them two or three times in an effort to pick up a word here, a bit of jargon there.

When two or more Latins get together the odds are that they will converse in Spanish. This has caused considerable resentment among American players, though not nearly as much as in earlier years. They feel that the moment we begin speaking Spanish we are talking about them. This is not so. We speak Spanish because it is our tongue and the words roll out without thought and we are free of the uneasiness that so often bothers us when we continually have to think about which word is right or wrong in English. I think that more and more American players are beginning to feel much more liberal and considerate about this situation.

Personally, I like the way it is summed up by Joe Garagiola, the world's foremost .257-hitting-catcher-turned-announcer. Garagiola, who is definitely not a Latin, says, "When these Latins talk English they have to stop and think about what they are going to say next. Immediately, though, when they see one of their own kind, they spit out their Spanish like a Viet Nam machine gun. I don't blame them; I would do the same thing. When the American ballplayers over in the Japanese leagues see one another I doubt that they get together and try to talk things over in Japanese."

Many of the other problems confronting Latin ballplayers have eased up in recent years, making it hard for some of us to fully appreciate the hardships that existed in earlier years. Not the least of the troubles centered around the racial situation. When Jackie Robinson came up to the Brooklyn Dodgers in 1947 he was said to have broken the color line in major league baseball. Was he *really* the first colored man to have played major league baseball? If colored meant being nonwhite, then Rafael Almeida and Armando Marsans, who played for the Cincinnati Reds 36 years before Jackie Robinson came along, should be credited with crashing the color barrier. Basing the issue strictly on skin pigmentation, why wasn't James Foy, an American Indian who broke in with Cleveland in the American Association in 1887, regarded as the first to cross the color line?

Baseball's unwritten law against admitting colored players was not so much against colored men as it was against American Negroes, for Almeida, Marsans and a flock of other Latins who came to the big leagues before 1947 were decidedly nonwhites. Down through the years there have been quite a few Latins who have been much darker than some of the American Negroes in the majors. Latins who came to the National and American Leagues before Jackie Robinson were definitely not regarded as whites and were frequently reminded of this.

Much of the story of the evolution of the Latin in baseball revolves around the Washington Senators, the first team to make extensive use of Latins. This came about largely because of the efforts of a man named Joe Cambria, known affectionately to Latins as Poppa Joe and kiddingly to one and all as Wet Wash Joe. He was Poppa Joe because he was the first person to really scout Latin players and because he did everything in his power to take care of them after signing them up. Poppa Joe had a shoulder that could be cried on, a wealth of helpful tips that could be relied on. He was Wet Wash Joe because he ran a laundry business in Baltimore. Wet Wash Joe was a man who could get your clothes clean, a man who could sign up Cuban prospects by the scads. He signed up so many of them that some of the Senator spring training camps in the 1940s looked like refugee stations. Most of those players had to be sent to the minor leagues, but others stuck with the Senators and they were the ones who cut the pathway to the majors that has been followed by hundreds of others since that time.

These Latins were not treated as equals by the whites. From opponents they got some of the most vociferous bench jockeying the game has ever known. From teammates they got cold shoulders, baseball's own version of icicles coated with frozen indifference and distrust. From the management they got the lowest wages that baseball law and a modified form of common decency would permit.

One of the early groups of Cubans who played with the Senators lived in a boardinghouse in Washington. One day a few white team-mates paid a visit to the boardinghouse. The landlady thought, "my land, it is so nice that these young gentlemen should come to pay a social visit to my guests." Then she heard a thump. Then there was a crash. Next came a bang, followed by a clatter, a boom, a crunch and a few howls of anguish. Just about then the landlady was beginning to suspect that the boys were not merely sitting around tell-ing jokes. Hard on the heels of these thoughts came the visiting play-ers, trooping out of the house now that their mission—to teach the Cubans a lesson because one of them had "forgotten his place"—had been completed.

A few years later, in 1944, the Cubans literally fought their way to a measure of respectability. This incident began when a husky 205-pound catcher from an opposing team began calling the Washington Cubans names that were not to be found anywhere in the little English pocket dictionaries that some of the players had purchased. Mike Guerra, a catcher for the Senators, told the critic to shut up. He did not, choosing rather to toss out a few more insults and to challenge Guerra, who was only 5 foot 9 and 150 pounds, to combat. Another of the Cubans on the Washington club, 6 foot 4 inch, 200-pound Roberto Ortiz, volunteered to intercede for Guerra. Reports on pre-cisely what took place vary, but it is clear that Ortiz flailed away with his fists and won a decisive victory over the loudmouthed opponent. One of the Cubans later commented proudly, "After that the rest of the players like us much more."

Even more beneficial than fisticuffs in the Latins' quest for accept-ance during the next two decades was the good-natured attitude of so many of these foreign players. Many Latins have a carefree, who-cares-if-the-house-is-burning-down-just-so-I-have-my-banjo-and-cigar outlook toward life. It is hard to dislike someone who is so cheerfully complacent. We all owe a great deal to such frolicsome *hombres* as Adolfo Luque, Connie Marrero, Minnie Minoso and Pedro Ramos, among many others. The natural wit of such players has done more for the cause of the Latins than perhaps anything else. Ebullient, wag-gish, comical men such as these have caused others to laugh, and when you can get a ballplayer to laugh you have taken a large step toward convincing him that you are human and worth befriending.

Despite his incendiary temper, Luque had a captivating personality and a gift for rendering a form of English that somehow came out more appealing than appalling. It was his hot-headedness that helped set off one of the better baseball brawls of the 1920s. Luque was pitching for the Cincinnati Reds at the time and took exception to the fact that one of the members of the New York Giants was calling him names that his parents had not christened him with.

When he had taken all he could, Luque calmly stood on the mound, took off his glove, placed the ball in it and put both on the ground. He then walked straight toward the Giant dugout and, without hesitation, walked right in and belted Casey Stengel (then a New York outfielder) right in the face. Stengel, who actually had not been the player who had been baiting Luque, retaliated with a punch of his own and a melee between the two clubs followed.

Once order was restored, Luque was banished from the game by the umpires. Soon after play had resumed another hassle broke out and when it did, Luque, armed with a bat, came rushing back onto the field. When this outbreak was settled, Luque was again ejected from the field. For many this would have been an inglorious day. Not for Luque, though. He was that rare type who set people off to talking about (1) how he had punched the wrong player, (2) how he had picked out Casey Stengel for his victim (Stengel was worth a laugh even in those days) and (3) how he had earned the distinction of having been ejected from the same game two times.

It was not until three days after his 43rd birthday that Luque appeared in his first World Series game. At that time he was doing his pitching for the Giants and he finally got his big chance when Manager Bill Terry brought him in to pitch in relief during the fifth game of the 1933 World Series against the Senators. New York went into the day with a 3-1 lead in games played and a need for only one more victory to clinch the World Championship. Luque came in with the score tied and, with his curve ball working almost as well as ever, gave up just two hits in four and one-third innings. Mel Ott homered in the top of the 10th inning to give the Giants a 4-3 lead, a lead that Luque appeared on the verge of blowing. After getting the first two men out, Luque gave up a single to Joe Cronin and a walk to Fred Schulte.

Terry walked out to the mound to have a few words with his ancient reliefer. The manager pointed out that the next hitter was Joe Kuhel, who had batted .322 that season and who was a lefthanded swinger, and that maybe a lefthanded pitcher like Carl Hubbell, who was warming up in the bullpen, would be more appropriate in this spot.

"I peetch," Luque said, settling the whole issue with two words. He then added one last thought, saying, "Beel, you listen to Poppa. I see you in the clawhouse queeck."

Three pitches later Kuhel had struck out, the Giants were champs and Luque saw Terry in the "clawhouse." For years thereafter, Terry got a big kick out of retelling the story of how Luque had described the big strikeout to him after the game. This is the way Luque, in his own patented version of English, told the tale:

"I look at thees Kool (Kuhel). I look hees feet. He ees stand 'way back. Ah! I peetch curve on outside corner. Umpire say strike! Ball come back. I take look around. Then I take quick look—quick—et Kool. Thees time I see hees feet is close by plate. Ah! I peetch curve inside corner. Umpire say strike! Ball come back. I look at bases. I look all around. I take quick look at Kool, hees feet. He ees move back again! I peetch curve outside. He sweeng and miss!"

Connie Marrero had a windup that looked like a cross between a windmill gone berserk and a mallard duck trying to fly backwards. Above all, he was known for two items of dress he was never without—a cigar and a smile, both as long and prominent as possible. Wherever Marrero went, laughter was soon to follow. He was that type of person and he did much to further the cause of the Latin.

Minnie Minoso was another person who had a captivating way. He used to talk about the days of his youth when he worked long hours in Cuba and when he was as slender as the sugar cane he used to cut down. When Minnie told the story he used to say, "I was very skin."

After being called out on a close play at second base by Umpire Charlie Berry, Minoso first sat, then kneeled on the bag. One of the players came over to ask if something was wrong. Minoso said, "No. I'm just praying for Charlie Berry." He once summed up his own philosophy on life by saying, "I never see anything impossible in life. I try to do good for everyone and be friends with everybody. No matter how hurt I am, I always try to laugh. That is my way."

Minoso was a fine hitter, a good outfielder, a hustler and had he not suffered some severe injuries he would have had well over 2,000 hits in his major league career. Manager Birdie Tebbetts claimed that Minnie caused a lot of baseball people to alter their thinking about the merits of being an opposite-field hitter. Minoso, a righthanded batter, excelled at hitting to right field and did so with power. "Everybody thought you had to be a pull-hitter to have power," Tebbetts says. "When Minnie came along and showed that he could hit for average and distance to all fields, people suddenly began taking opposite-field hitters seriously." They also began taking Latins a little more seriously.

Willie Miranda, a slick-fielding Cuban shortstop, found that being able to speak some English had its drawbacks. He tells his story like this:

"I spoke better than most players when I was with Washington, so they wanted me to help them. I say, 'Fine, I help you all I can.' But then they start calling me all the time and walking in and out of my room all day and all night. I couldn't get any sleep. Consuegra calls me one morning and wakes me up. He says to me in Spanish, 'I can't shave.'

" 'Why not?' I ask him.

" 'I don't have any blades.'

" 'Go downstairs and buy some,' I tell him.

" 'I can't.'

" 'Why not?'

" 'I don't know how to ask for them.'

" 'Point,' I say to him.

" 'I'm afraid to.'

" 'Okay, come up and shave with my stuff.' "

It is not always easy for a Latin to be in good spirits. He is in a strange land working under considerable pressure, spending part or maybe even all of the season away from wife, children or other loved ones and in some cases is kept continually on edge because he is from a country that is rife with oppression or sickness or where revolutions are always a danger. As much as he enjoys playing baseball, Minoso used to concoct assorted stories about why he couldn't get to spring training on time. The best at that, though, was Miranda. When he was late reporting from his home in Cuba to the Baltimore Oriole spring training base one year, he finally replied to the club's frantic pleas by explaining that, "I can't get to America because I'm having trouble getting my parakeet through customs."

The plight of the Cuban has been a sad one since Fidel Castro and communism took over the nation. Cuban players no longer have a homeland they can return to after the season. Some of them, including Pedro Ramos lost quite a bit of property when Castro took over.

"In Cuba I had a cigar factory," Ramos begins his story. "I give money to my father to start in the cigar business. We sell cigars called *El Gladiator* that have a picture of me in a baseball uniform right on the cigar band. Our business gets going pretty good and then Castro comes along and says that no one can have a business of his own. Soon everybody is working for the government.

"It is hard to get out of Cuba now and baseball is now just a game there, not a future anymore for the young ones. Not so much interest in baseball there now. Lots of boys used to say, 'I want to play in the U.S.' Castro says this baseball is a monopoly in the U.S. He says it should be like in Russia. I think a man should have a chance to prove himself."

Ramos is the sort who, with the wink of an eye and a slight change of voice inflection, can veer off into more pleasant topics. For Pedro there is nothing more pleasant to discuss than his fascination with

117

cowboys and pistols. He reads Cuban cowboy books by the dozen. One day he got to talking about the latest book he was reading. It was a book by Marcial Lafuente Estefania, with Tex Mirror cast as the hero. Talking about this book, Ramos said, "Mirror is a good guy who is fast with the gun, but he doesn't want to kill anybody. But this one guy he tries to kill him, so he has to shoot in self-defense and he kills the man. Now the man's—the one who was killed—three brothers come after the good guy and they chase him. I'm on page 12 now."

Ramos carries in his wallet a picture taken of himself when he was decked out in full Western garb during the shooting of a Cuban television western. "I was a Texas man," Ramos explained. "That was before Castro. I have maybe a dozen cowboy shirts, some very fancy. I have four, five pairs of boots, belts, hats, pants and much guns."

How good a shot is Pedro? "Pretty fast, but I never miss," he says. "Kirkland (Outfielder Willie Kirkland) he doesn't think I can shoot. So in Arizona once at the park he puts an orange in the tree. I draw my pistol and shoot the orange. He thinks this is maybe lucky so he puts up a paper cup. I shoot that. He says to me, 'You are crazy.' Many people like to play golf. I like to shoot. Maybe now that CBS owns the Yankees I can get a job as cowboy of some of the television programs. I like that."

Although a good sense of humor has helped the Latin cause out of some tight spots, it would be foolish to insist that all Latins are lovable and that they have endeared themselves to other players so completely that there has never been a flat tire along the road to acceptance. One of our most significant and costly stumblingblocks has been the Latin temperament, a napalm-type disposition that can erupt at any time, any place and for any reason. This instant temper has left some singed areas here and there around the baseball leagues, both major and minor.

A Roberto Ortiz may well have gained greater respect for the early band of Latins when he proved that he knew how to use his fists. Still, had each of us tried similar tactics we would have defeated our own cause. A fellow countryman of mine, Pitcher Juan Marichal of the San Francisco Giants, lost his temper in a game near the end of the 1965 season and swung his bat at the head of Los Angeles Catcher John Roseboro and, regrettably, connected.

This is not typical of Latin behavior; our self-control is generally better than that. The Latin temper — that ever-burning ember — is such, however, that some hasty, angry words have been spoken at inopportune times. Here it is important to point out two things: (1) that Latins have attained the degree of acceptance that permits them to speak as freely as they do and (2) that it is unlikely that Latin tempers are really much worse than American tempers. One fact that Latins must never forget is that as ballplayers, we were, are, and always will be, foreigners in America and we cannot hope that we will ever be totally accepted.

A few years ago my temper went skyward faster than a kite on a windy day. What set it off was a notification from former Baseball Commissioner Ford Frick that I had been fined $250. Among the factors in this complicated affair was the failure of the political leadership in the Dominican Republic during the fall of 1962 and the failure of Frick. Because of the political unrest in my land, the government felt that it had to try something to calm down the people. The best tension-relieving device that could be thought of was to hold a three-game series between baseball teams from the Dominican Republic and Cuba in Santo Domingo. The reasoning was that a few hours at the ballpark would divert the minds of the Dominican people from thoughts of revolution, riot and mayhem. Even the most rabid of the political reactionaries was willing to take an afternoon or two or three (the games were not to be played at night, as they normally would have been, because of the government-enforced curfew) away from their submachine guns and hand grenades. These heavily armed men and boys apparently figured that they could have a revolt any ol' time, but a baseball game, well, that was something else. Many of them came to the games, their weapons held in their laps or bulging from their pockets. I kept hoping that no one would yell, "Kill the umpire!"

When Commissioner Frick heard that several major leaguers intended to take part in this three-game series, he denied us permission to do so. All the players had already gathered in Santo Domingo when word filtered down that Frick had said he would levy fines against any and all big league players who participated in the games. A quick call was put through to Dr. Rafael Bonelli, the president of the country. Bonelli wasted no time in stating that, "I am the president of the Dominican Republic and I say that it is all right to play."

With the backing of the president and with 22,000 people in the stands for the first game, there was no way that Ford Frick could scare us out of playing. If we didn't play there would have been a revolt right on the spot and we would have been prime targets. Once Frick found out that we had disobeyed him and taken part in the games, he sent a message notifying me that I had been fined. Most of the other big league players who were involved received similar greetings.

Frick, who never understood the Latins and their problems, had no

119

concept of the political consequences of the three-game series, nor did he have any idea that once the games had been set up there was no way the Dominican people would have permitted big leaguers from their country not to compete. We could have been threatened with $1,000,000 fines by Frick and there still would not have been any way for us to have avoided playing—unless we were willing to risk bodily harm.

When I received the cable from Frick informing me that he was assessing me $250 for playing against the Cubans, I wadded it up into a tight ball and threw it as hard as I could. Added to the fine was the threat that if I did not ante up I would be denied the privilege of playing baseball in the United States in 1963. One of the first semi-clear thoughts that crossed my mind after my initial anger had subsided, was that I would take a firm stand and would not pay the fine, even if it meant that I would not be permitted to play baseball.

This all took place during November of 1962. By the time I had reported to the new Giant spring training camp in Casa Grande, Arizona, I had been warned by Frick that failure to pay the $250 meant forfeiture of the right to play. I remained adamant. The first real jolt to my campaign came when Giant front office executives informed me that, because of Frick's ruling, they could not and would not even give me a uniform until the fine was paid in full. As I watched teammates suit up, I got the first inkling of what it might be like not to pull on a uniform for an entire season.

All that was needed, though, was a quick pep talk with myself to furnish me with renewed strength for my battle. After three days of this, the Giants told me that they would pay the fine for me. I told them no, that I would pay it myself, for it was becoming evident to me that my crusade, forged in the heat of anger, was actually subsisting more on stubbornness than on common sense at that point. Frick, I knew, had not acted without reason and even though I felt he was wrong I respected him as Commissioner. I paid the fine and quickly suited up.

Throughout my campaign I had voiced the opinion that Latin ballplayers were misunderstood and would remain misunderstood until we had some representation in the office of the commissioner of baseball. Revolutionists in America some 200 years earlier used to shout at their British overlords that, "Taxation without representation is tyranny." I could sympathize with those revolutionists, feeling as I did that Latin ballplayers were being fined, were being abused and were not being given a proper audience because there was no one in the commissioner's office to represent us.

News came in early December, 1965 that Bobby Maduro had been hired by William D. Eckert, the new commissioner of baseball, to handle the affairs of Latin ballplayers. With the news came a sense of relief and the feeling that one of our biggest needs had been taken care of. Having a representative in such a position was cause for elation, but having a man as capable as Maduro as our spokesman was almost too good to be true. Maduro is a Cuban, a gentleman and a man who has been in baseball for more than 20 years. Just a few years ago he was the owner of the Havana Sugar Kings of the International League. He knows Latins; he knows ballplayers; he knows baseball. We couldn't ask for a better man.

Not even a Bobby Maduro can step in, wave a wand and make all the woes vanish, however. It was late in August of 1966 that Roberto Clemente of the Pittsburgh Pirates created a number of headlines when he stated that, "The Latin American player doesn't get the recognition he deserves. Neither does the Negro player . . . unless he does something really spectacular, like Willie Mays. We have self-satisfaction, yes. But after the season is over nobody cares about us."

Clemente then went into further detail as he spilled out his feelings to the Associated Press. "Zoilo Versalles (a Cuban) was the Most Valuable Player in the American League, but how many times has he been asked to make appearances at dinners or meetings during the winter? Juan Marichal (a Dominican) is one of the greatest pitchers in the game, but does he get invited to banquets?

"Somebody say we live too far away. That's a lousy excuse. It cost $90 round trip by air from Puerto Rico to New York. It cost more from California. And Versalles lives in Minnesota; so does Tony Oliva (the two-time American League batting champion from Cuba)."

Clemente, who lives in Puerto Rico, didn't stop at this point. "I am an American citizen," he went on to say. "I live 250 miles from Miami. But some people think I live in the jungle. To the people in the States we are outsiders, foreigners. We get together sometimes and we talk about it. We are not happy about it. This is a matter of sports . . . of a man's ability and his accomplishments. What matters what language he speaks best?"

Roberto, I feel, was right in much of what he said. There are some delicate matters to be considered here and I believe it is important that Latin ballplayers should always keep in mind that, as Clemente himself points out, "we are outsiders, foreigners." Total acceptance is something that most likely will never be accorded us. Clemente is right in saying that the Marichals, Olivas and other leading Latins are not given nearly as many chances to make some money on the banquet circuit as some lesser known American ballplayers are. Here, I think, another basic fact must not be overlooked. Baseball is a business. It is played clean, it is played hard, it is played beautifully, yet at the heart of the game is the money that keeps it going and makes it a very big business.

This business aspect drifts over into the winter banquet circuit. Latins are affected because so many of us speak a halting or broken English. It would be bad business to hire speakers who cannot express themselves clearly and it would be worse business to hire them when there are highly talented Americans who are available. The same is true with getting endorsements and making commercials; when the time comes to pick the player who will help sell the most, the advertiser must select the one who will do the best job.

Another area in which the Latin has not done well financially is that of bonuses. Bonuses were given out in such liberal doses for a few years that unless you got $100,000 or more you had to hang your head in shame. While all this big spending was going on, young Latin prospects were scrambling to get enough of a bonus to buy a suit of clothes. Big money simply was not given to Latins. I was a little irked by this until I realized some of the circumstances. To begin with, a bonus is based on a boy's ability while he is yet an amateur, and on the potential he has for the future. Most Latin boys at age 17, 18, 19 are very slight in build when compared to the average American. Furthermore, the Latin hasn't had much chance to accomplish a great deal in baseball. He is, for the most part, an unknown quantity. American youths grow up with baseball and can participate in all sorts of leagues from the day they are old enough to swing a bat until they are ready to be put on the baseball auction block.

One example of the Latin situation is my brother Matty. When the Giants signed him he was about 5 foot 5 and weighed about 130 pounds. He had exhibited no particular talent as a baseball player back home and the only reason he was even given a contract was because he was my brother. Matty hit only .247 in his first year as a Class D player, but he kept growing and the Giants did not give up on him. He has turned out to be an exceptional hitter, something that no one had any way of knowing when he was a scrawny teenager. I received a meager $200 bonus and, truthfully, that was all I was worth because I simply had not played enough baseball for anyone to tell whether I had talent or not.

Less than one month after the 1966 season ended, the Atlanta Braves issued their 40-man roster for the following year: Eight of the players, a full 20 per cent of the squad, were Latins from five different countries—Cuba, the Bahamas, the Dominican Republic, Puerto Rico and Venezuela. To me that was indicative of the progress made by Latin ballplayers in the major leagues.

CHAPTER 14

BASEBALL FROM SPRING THROUGH WINTER

Spring training is a dreary time. There are kinks in muscles that haven't been used in months, there are lots of calisthenics and there is the constant refrain from coaches to, "Run. Get out there and run laps." Once I overheard a pitcher on another club being chastised by a coach. When the pitcher, dripping with perspiration, stopped running laps, the coached yelled at him, "If you don't keep running, your legs will give out this season."

"And if I do keep on running," the pitcher replied, "my mind will give out."

Adding to the burden of spring training is the playing schedule, which calls for a game almost every day. In 1963 there were long bus rides from Phoenix to Tucson, Mesa and Apache Junction, Arizona and plane trips to the Los Angeles Angel camp in Palm Springs, California. Luckily, there were enough diversions to bring relief to the otherwise bleak six weeks of practice. Just as the fans watch us, we often watch them.

Ladies come to these spring games with their knitting. Men peel off their shirts to bask in the sun. Dogs trot across the field during games. It's all part of the fun of spring training. One woman in Phoenix didn't think it was all so funny. She was part of an overflow crowd that watched one of our games against the Indians. To accommodate the large turnout, a section of left field was roped off, with the fans being allowed to stand behind the rope. In the fourth inning McCovey hit a long drive that landed among that cluster of fans behind the rope. To be exact, it landed right on top of a woman's head. McCovey got a ground-rule double; the woman got a king-size lump. We were afraid that she was more seriously hurt than it appeared. She was led from the field to get some treatment and it was decided that, as a precautionary measure, she should be taken to the hospital. After she had waited about 20 minutes at the park, a local policeman told her "The ambulance hasn't arrived yet, but if you'd like we can take you to the hospital in a police car or a hearse."

It's always fun to watch the kids at the parks. What amazes me is how so many of them can attend games during school hours. In Mesa, where the Cubs train, the boys form partnerships in the unending quest for foul balls. One of the partners will buy a ticket to the game and then stand on the top row of seats and point and yell whenever and wherever a foul ball is going out of the park. Once the signal is given, the rush is on, with some 15 or 20 boys in pursuit of the bouncing, ricocheting ball. Their work is hazardous because they have to patrol an area that has a lot of traffic. They dodge around moving cars and dive headlong over and under parked cars to get those balls. In addition, they come up with many a torn shirt and skinned knee.

In Apache Junction, where the Houston club used to train, the boys were a little more farsighted. Most of the foul balls landed in a rocky parking lot, so many of the boys wore protective head guards—everything from football helmets to army helmets. A few, too young to appreciate the meaning of monthly installment payments and the labor that goes into polishing a car, stood on the hoods or tops of automobiles to wait for fouls.

Other boys work on the scoreboards, posting the large metal numerals that give the score inning by inning. Or at least that is what they are supposed to do. In the delightful nonconformity of spring training, the score sometimes is not posted for two or three innings because the boys are taking a Coke break. We played the Indians in Tucson one day when the scoreboard boy posted the wrong score early in the game and did not get it correct until the ninth inning.

Some of the fun in Palm Springs was provided by Irv Kaze, then the Angel publicity man. Conditions had to be just right, however. To pull off his gag, Kaze had to wait until a foul ball went right over the press box towards a lot full of cars. When this happened, Kaze would switch on the public address system and dump the remains of a broken bottle into a metal container that was held right next to the microphone. If a responsive crowd was on hand, more than a few worried car owners would jump up to check on their windshields.

Probably the strangest thing that happened in the spring of 1963 was Tito Francona of the Indians hitting a home run that helped solve a murder. Tito says that he recalled having read about a murder in the Tucson area. The police apparently had a good idea who the killer was but were unable to track him down. Then Francona, who also says that as he read the story he thought that it shouldn't be too hard to find the killer, hit a home run that landed in some tall grass outside the park. When some people went to look for the ball, they found a body as well. It turned out to be the suspected killer, who had committed suicide.

One of the really courageous stories about spring training concerns a 17-year-old boy named Manuel Enrique Hernandez Gazmuri. In

July of 1962, Gazmuri started a circuitous route to spring training that began in his native Cuba. Before leaving his homeland, Gazmuri had already become a national hero. Fidel Castro had proclaimed Gazmuri, an almost unbeatable lefthanded pitcher at home, as a model for all Cuban youth. For his exemplary attitude and ability, Gazmuri was given a house by Castro. It was the home of former major league pitcher Sandy Consuegra, who lost his property when he chose the freedom of the United States rather than communism. Gazmuri rejected the gift.

In the back of Gazmuri's mind was a plan to reach America. Somehow, the Castro government found out about the plan. Gazmuri was labeled a traitor and a guard was assigned to keep watch over him. Word leaked through to Gazmuri that several compatriots had devised a means of escape. Stealthily, Gazmuri joined them and they made their way to the ocean and pushed off in a 16-foot rowboat that night. Their destination was Florida.

Despite a clean getaway, there were still many trying moments ahead. There was hardly any food for the small band of men, nothing more than a jug of water, a can of meat and some chocolate. Gazmuri did not eat anything on the trip, but he did share in bailing out the leaky boat and, like his friends, he felt a sudden skip of his heart on each of three occasions when their five-horsepower motor conked out. Once in Florida, Gazmuri contacted a baseball scout he knew, Julio (Monchy) DeArcos of the Cleveland Indians. The Indians signed him up and even though he pitched just a few innings in the Eastern League that summer, they thought so highly of him that they placed him on their major league roster and brought him to their spring training camp in 1963.

Two weeks before spring training began for us that year, Al Dark took part in the National Baseball Players' Golf Championship in Miami. In addition to being the defending champion, Dark was trying to win the tournament for a record fifth time. He came close, finishing in third place, just two strokes in back of Jim Hearn, a former pitcher and teammate on the Giants during the 1950s. Dark's loss in Miami was to be one of his lesser disappointments in 1963.

At the end of spring training our team had the worst record in the National League. Our 10 wins and 17 defeats left us six games behind Houston and five in back of New York, the two weakest teams in the league. Spring training won-lost results are generally regarded as meaningless—especially by those who haven't done well. Thus, it was encouraging for us to open the regular season with a 9-2 win over the Colts in Houston, where the temperature that day rose to 90 degrees. I enjoy warm weather and during our three games, all of which we won, I had two homers among my eight hits in 12 times up. At the end of April my batting average was .392. After that it was all downhill, for my average tumbled quickly. We stayed in the scramble for the pennant until September 1st, when the first-place Dodgers defeated us and left us seven and a half games in their wake.

Jesus was called up to the Giants in September after hitting .324 for Tacoma in the Pacific Coast League. Now there were three Alous on the Giants. On September 10th we all went to bat in the same inning, which must surely have been a record. None of us could hit the ball out of the infield in that inning, however. Less than two weeks later, at the Polo Grounds, we set a more dignified mark when all three Giant outfield positions were manned by Alous; Matty was in left, Jesus in right and I was in center. Collectively, we had four hits that day—two singles for Jesus, a double and triple for me.

In our final game of the season, I had two hits, one a home run, and drove in three runs as we beat Pittsburgh 4-2. That left me with final hitting statistics that showed a .281 average, 20 home runs and 82 runs batted in. That, plus our third-place finish, 11 games to the rear of the pennant-winning Dodgers, made it a frustrating season all around.

Two events occurred in the next few months, however, that kept the year 1963 from being a complete washout for me. One was the most exciting thing ever to happen to me in baseball, the other was the most shocking. The first took place in a Dominican League game against crosstown rival Licey. To appreciate the impact of this event, you must understand that the rivalry between Licey and Escogido can be likened only to the Dodger-Giant feud. Licey was leading us 5-4 in the seventh inning. I was on first base with one of the three hits I had that night, but there seemed little hope of scoring. There were two men out and Joe Sparks, the batter, had a count of no balls and two strikes on him. I figured he would be swinging at the next pitch, so I took off for second base. The pitch was a ball, but my tactics so surprised everybody that the shortstop and second baseman did little more than watch me steal the base. On the next pitch, which I felt Sparks would be swinging at, I stole third base. That pitch, too, had been a ball. Now, with the count 2 and 2, I took off for home plate, even though I was positive that Sparks would be taking a cut at the pitch. He didn't swing. The pitch was a ball and I slid under the catcher's tag to score the tying run. As the crowd gave me a big ovation, I could only be thankful that I had somehow stolen three bases on three pitches on which I had guessed wrong each time. The real payoff came when Sparks, finally swinging at a 3-and-2 pitch, hit a game-winning home run.

About six weeks later, on December 3rd, I arose early and took off on one of my all-day fishing trips in my rowboat. It was almost 5 in the evening before I returned home and one look at Maria was enough to tell me that something was wrong.

"They traded you," Maria called to me even before I got to the house.

Those three words reverberated in my mind and I could feel myself rock back on my heels, as though hit by a blow. There was a sudden pain and it was a few seconds before I could ask, "To what team?"

"Milwaukee," Maria said.

"That's not too bad," was my halfhearted reply. For a few minutes I tried to fight back inwardly, much as a person does when he is trying not to give into ether on the operating table. That was followed by a submission to the knowledge that I was helpless in this situation. Suddenly, a fury welled up within me as deep resentment took hold. Then I slumped inwardly, realizing that this was one thing over which I had no control. It is hard to say whether my feelings were those of embarrassment or hurt pride, but whatever they were I know that the only comforting thought I had during those first minutes of doubt was the realization that this trade must have been the Lord's will for me. There was no escaping my own desire, though, and I knew that I disliked the city of Milwaukee more than any other in the league. I even thought about quitting the game rather than play there.

Gone were the dreams of playing in the same outfield with Matty and Jesus. Gone were the close friendships I had made with so many Giant teammates and friends in San Francisco. Gone were the scrambles for the pennant, at least for the coming year. Milwaukee had finished in sixth place, 15 games behind Los Angeles, in 1963. Then, as I set aside my disappointment and let the Lord take over, I could see that all was not so bad. If He wanted me in Milwaukee, then there must be a reason for it, I thought.

Along with me, the Giants sent Catcher Ed Bailey, Pitcher Billy Hoeft and Infielder Ernie Bowman to the Braves in exchange for Pitchers Bob Shaw and Bob Hendley and Catcher Del Crandall. It was a trade in which the Giants sought to get some of the pitching strength they so badly needed. The more I pondered the deal, the more I wondered if there were other reasons why the Giants had traded me. Had the Giants resented my leadership of the Latin faction on the club? I was not a leader in any formal sense, but I probably did serve as a spokesman for the Latins on our team, a role I did not particularly enjoy. Had the Giants resented my speaking out concerning their treatment, or, as I felt, mistreatment, of Matty after he had been hurt? Matty had been injured during spring training in 1963 and

I felt that the condition of his left knee warranted more medical care than he received. There was one game in which we were leading by a dozen runs and Matty, ailing knee and all, was sent into center field to replace Willie Mays. Then, instead of sending Matty to a specialist, the Giants shipped him to the minors, hardly the place to have torn ligaments repaired. As a result of his injury, Matty hit only .145 for the Giants and played in just 25 games in the minors. About two weeks after my trade, Matty was in New York for an operation on his knee, which he had reinjured during the Dominican League season.

As the winter wore on, I began to think that perhaps the constant elbow trouble I had had in windy and cold San Francisco might not bother me so much in Milwaukee. I also began looking forward to playing on a team with such hitters as Hank Aaron and Eddie Mathews.

Opening Day of the 1964 season was a bad day for me in many ways. On the morning of our game with the Giants, I was walking around San Francisco when I somehow ripped the inside seam of my trousers. Fortunately, I was carrying some clothes on a hanger and was able to cover myself up. Still, I had to go back to the hotel and change and, as a result, missed the team bus to Candlestick Park for my first game as a Brave. Bragan used me as his center fielder and leadoff man, which was fine with me. One thing I couldn't quite get used to, however, was which dugout to go to at the end of each inning. Time after time I would run from center field after the third out of an inning and head for the first base dugout, which is where the Giants were located and which was where I had been going for the past five and a half seasons. I had just a single that day as we lost to the Giants, who hit five home runs. When I played my first game in Milwaukee a few days later, it was the Giants who once again were our opponents. Again I had one hit, which was not much help, for the Giants, with Willie McCovey hitting three home runs, defeated us 8-6.

There were many losses during those early months of the season and we had to labor hard to stay in the first division. My lack of hitting didn't help either. Bragan, understandably, moved me from one spot in the batting order to another, benched me, put me back in the lineup, switched me from center field to first base. One day, shortly after being shifted to first base, I twisted my right knee during a workout. I had to be helped from the field, but I was certain I would be back in the lineup in a jiffy. My prognosis couldn't have been much more incorrect, so maybe it was a good thing that I hadn't become a doctor after all. Two days after hurting my knee I underwent surgery. That was on June 26th in Milwaukee.

There have been many times during my life when I have been worried, doubtful and discouraged and it was during the early days of my convalescence that I felt more deeply ensnared by these attitudes than ever. "See," I began saying to myself ,"I knew I shouldn't be playing for Milwaukee. How could I have been traded from San Francisco, where I had become active in church work and seemed to be doing so well? Why, in San Francisco I had been speaking weekly, sometimes, twice a week or more, to youth groups, church gatherings and businessmen's organizations. In Milwaukee I am lost and now I am injured." My indignation was more selfish than it was righteous.

A few days later there began a transformation in my outlook. Mail came from everywhere—get-well cards from fans, notes from friends and many, many letters of encouragement from fellow Christians, some of whom I knew, some of whom I did not know. Al Worthington, ever faithful to me, wrote. Bobby Richardson of the Yankees sent a letter. Don Rood pointed out that there surely was a reason for my injury and that the Lord would sustain me. These cards and letters meant much to me and as I read them over and over I could feel my wrath melt away. These good people had taken time to remember me. More important, I saw that the Lord was not about to forsake me in my plight. For the first time since I had been traded, I entrusted myself fully to His care. I almost had to laugh at the futility I had experienced during the first two months of the season, a period in which I had not been relying on the Lord as I should have been. My six home runs and .253 average typified the utter failure of my efforts.

There were many thoughts that crossed my mind while I was in the hospital during the next few weeks. One of the most predominant had to do with the courage of ballplayers I had known who had also been injured. For the first time in my life I sympathized with what Mickey Mantle of the Yankees had been going through so many years. To be honest, I had never felt sorry for Mantle, a player who was being paid $100,000 a year. His injuries, I had thought, were unfortunate, but I felt he was lucky to be earning the money he was. Now that I was undergoing the sort of physical problems that Mantle had known for years, I finally appreciated his courage. In the years since then I have seen Mantle suffer through even more adversity. One spring he looked so wobbly that it seemed that there should have been a couple of players out there just to hold him in place while he tried to swing the bat.

As I lay in bed I had to ask myself some questions and, above all, had to seek some honest answers. Did I really want to play baseball? My first answer was a quick yes. As I thought more about this my answer became a stronger yes. Since 1956 I had been playing the game almost year-round and now that I was away from it I found that I longed for it more than ever. It wasn't so much that I wanted to make a name for myself as it was that I saw the good things about the game, its virtues as a character builder and foundation for life. When I asked myself if I felt that this was where God wanted me, my reply was again yes. As a ballplayer I had found that the outreach of my Christian testimony was greater than it would be in any other area. I was not endowed with the ability to be a preacher or pastor, yet I knew that a certain number of people—especially youngsters—were willing to listen to what I had to say merely because I was a big league player. I could see that if I wanted to help people I could best do it by establishing myself as a ballplayer. Having answered yes to these two questions, I knew that I would have to be willing to rededicate myself to the Lord and His work and that I would have to seek His will and not mine. This meant that I would have to yield more of myself to Him and once having decided upon this course I prayed that I would be unswerving toward Him in my obedience.

While I was in the hospital, my leg was in a cast. The muscles in my leg got weak and when the cast was removed, I was appalled to find that the leg had actually become much smaller. Now that the injury and the operation were over with, there came the work of rebuilding the leg. It takes a lot of work to develop muscles properly and to get them to function on command. There were exercises to be done daily and, when the leg was strong enough, lots of running to be done. I recall running around the beach at Lake Michigan, plodding mile after mile and having people stare at me. I was finding out, probably just as Mantle had, that all the will power a man can summon cannot heal a damaged leg overnight. There were more exercises to be done and more miles to be run.

It seemed as though the Lord was teaching me about the frailty of the human body. All my life I had been in good physical condition, had never been a smoker or drinker and had taken care of myself. Now, however, the Lord was showing me that there were weaknesses in my body, just as there are weaknesses in all men. Aside from a tonsilectomy, my knee operation had been my first real experience with surgery.

Many people felt that I would not be able to play again that year, but within five weeks after my injury, I was back in uniform and a few days after that, I was in the starting lineup. I had just one hit in my first 17 at bats after taking over at first base again and on September 4th my batting average was down to .231. Bragan stuck with me, however, and the hits started to come. Against the Mets on September 10th I hit my first home run since being hurt. I also hit a double in the ninth inning to beat the Mets 7-6. There is nothing like a game-winning hit to revive a hitter and a few days later I had a three-run homer to defeat the Cubs 5-2. Our club perked up too, winning games in September, a closing rush that gave us a fifth-place finish just five games back of the pennant-winning St. Louis Cardinals. In my last 44 times up I had 17 hits—a .386 average—and that, plus the team's spurt at the end of the season, raised my spirits considerably. That finishing kick also raised my average at the end of the year to .253 and brought my RBI total up to 51. Those statistics weren't impressive, but after what I had been through I was thankful that I was able to play at all.

It was a calamitous year for all the Alous. Matty's left wrist was fractured by a pitch thrown by Bob Veale of the Pirates. Jesus played fairly regularly for the Giants, but suffered a severe spike wound on his foot and wound up with only a .274 average. I suffered an added indignity that year. It came shortly after I returned to the Braves following my injury. Bragan had sent me in as a pinch hitter against the Cardinals in a game in which we were well in front. Bob Humphreys was the St. Louis pitcher and he threw me three fastballs right down the middle of the plate. I was so rusty that I didn't swing at any of them. Augie Donatelli, the home plate umpire, correctly called me out on strikes. As I walked away from the plate I threw my helmet and bat on the ground in disgust. I noticed that the helmet took an odd bounce behind me and as I turned around I noticed that it almost hit Donatelli, who immediately threw me out of the game.

"How can you throw me out?" I asked him. "I didn't protest your calls."

"You almost hit me," Donatelli said.

"I apologize. I didn't mean it."

"You're making the game look bad by doing that kind of thing," he said.

When I got back to the bench I had to explain to some of my teammates, who couldn't figure out what was going on, why I had been ejected from the game. That is the only time in my career that I have been thrown out of a game and I still feel bad about it. I would like to have been able to say that I had never been thumbed out of a game. When I noticed that the date was September 3rd it seemed fitting, in an incongruous way, that I should have been so humiliated on what was the 34th anniversary of the worst hurricane ever to strike the Dominican Republic.

There was still one more embarrassment for me to suffer through in 1964. The United States State Department sent a goodwill baseball team to tour Latin America after the major league season. On the team were such players as Lee Maye, Chuck Cottier, Jimmie Hall, Ronnie Kline and Mike de la Hoz. The team travelled all over South America and wherever they went they were greeted warmly—until they got to Santo Domingo. There they were called names and had stones thrown at them. What embarrassed me most was that this took place at the high school I had attended as a youngster. This incident was an outbreak of anti-American feeling and the players had to leave the school grounds as fast as they could. Reid Cabral, then the president of the country, informed the group that they could hold a clinic the next day and that he would guarantee them the protection of the army. Wisely, the players said thanks, but no thanks and got out of the country. I had to hang my head in shame.

As I reviewed the year, though, I saw that I had a great deal to be grateful for. Most of all, I felt closer to the Lord than I had ever been. I also felt that the thinking I had done during my convalescence had enabled me to understand myself more fully. And, in Houston, late in the season, I had taken part in what had been called the Latin American Baptist New Life Crusade, an evangelistic effort that was being conducted throughout Texas. It was there that I met a Reverend Rudy Hernandez, who, like me, had been raised a Catholic. Our bond was not an outgrowth of our Catholic heritage, but rather an offshoot of our desire to reach those people to whom Christ was a stranger.

When I got home to the Dominican Republic after the season, I did a lot of running to strengthen my leg. I would run 8, 10, maybe 12 miles in the morning and then go back to the beaches to run through the sand for another session later in the day. As the winter went on, my leg felt stronger and stronger. Matty and Jesus, too, were healthy now and there was a two-game span during the Dominican League season when the three of us had a total of 17 hits.

As always, I received my contract for the next season in January and I was pleasantly surprised by the consideration that the Braves showed me. They offered me the same salary as the year before, which, in light of my injury, was most kind of them. In addition to having been hurt and ineffective in 1964, I understood that my surgery, medical and hospital bills had cost the Braves some $3,000. I had anticipated a cut in pay and gladly signed the contract sent by General Manager John McHale, vowing that I would earn every penny.

Getting ready to go to spring training is the hardest time of the year for me. As the day of departure comes closer I can't help thinking that soon I will be leaving behind my family, my friends, and the hills, ocean and mountains that I love so much. As soon as I find out when I am to report to spring training I buy my plane ticket. When the time comes to leave, I always find that my first ordeal is that of mental preparation, for I know that once I board that plane it is time to concentrate on baseball. I force myself not to think too much about my family and my country and begin turning my thoughts to baseball. This is not to say that I don't think about those people and things that I have left behind. To play my best, though, I have found that I cannot afford to let my mind be in the Dominican Republic at the same time that my body is at the ball park.

My most important chore during spring training in 1965 was to prove that my leg was in good shape and that I could run, hit and field as well as before. My leg turned out to be okay and I felt that I had a fairly good spring and a respectable season, as well, in 1965. Bragan shifted me around from the outfield to first base but kept me in the leadoff spot most of the time. In June I had six runs batted in during one game and in July I led off successive games with first-inning homers. The year was not without its slumps, unfortunately. This time, though, I did not waste away on the bench when I was taken out of the lineup. I managed to get my first pinch hit home runs. The first came off Bob Buhl of the Cubs in a losing cause, but my second one beat Jack Fisher and the Mets. In between, I had a pinch-single that started a game-winning rally against the Pirates. Not all of my time on the bench resulted from slumps, though. For about three weeks, around midseason, I was bothered by a pulled muscle in my left leg. Bragan was in need of a pinch hitter one day so he called on me, gimpy leg and all. I hit the ball right back to John Tsitouris, the Cincinnati pitcher, who evidently forgot that I had a bad leg. He could have rolled the ball to first base and had me out by 20 steps. Instead, Tsitouris hurried his throw and it sailed past first base and far down the right field line. A decent runner would easily have made it to second base or possibly third on the overthrow. I barely made it to first base and then was taken out for a pinch runner, who scored the first run of what turned out to be a big rally.

When the season ended, I had 23 home runs and 78 runs batted in, and my .297 average placed me 13th in the league in batting. One point ahead of me was Jesus, who had been among the top 10 hitters until the final weeks. Matty had started the season very well, then was hampered by assorted ailments and problems, and finished up at .231. When the Giants were in need of pitching help late in the season, Matty, who has a good arm and throws a dandy curve ball, was used as a relief pitcher against the Pirates. Matty struck out three of the six batters he faced in two innings. San Francisco finished in second place, two games behind Los Angeles. Milwaukee came in fifth, 11 games out of first place.

The Dominican Republic had been a cauldron of unrest all year, so I kept my family with me throughout the season instead of sending them home in September as I had done in previous years. I had no idea how my parents were while I was in America. Mail service within the Dominican Republic was almost nonexistent and, despite three months of trying, I had not been able to get a call through to my folks. It was a relief to get home and find that everyone was well. My parents had moved to Santo Domingo, but my father spent most of his time tending to the farm in Haina.

Knowing that the situation at home was worse than ever because of the latest revolt and knowing that there might not be a chance to play winter ball, I took quite a bit of money with me when I left America. Many of my friends and relatives were in need and I felt compelled to help them out as much as possible. I wasn't trying to set myself up as a soft touch; it was simply that I felt obligated to lend a hand to those people who had helped me in the past.

Because of the dangers in my country, plans for the winter league were muddled. We were not allowed to play under the mantle of organized baseball and no American players were permitted to compete in the Dominican Republic, according to rulings handed down by the baseball commissioner's office. There were enough native players who wanted to organize a league, so we formed the Federation of Dominican Players. We didn't have enough players for the usual four-team league but when we got the season underway in late November we had three pretty good clubs. Attendance at our games was, as in past years, excellent. There were some 17,000 people at the opening game. It wasn't long, however, before attendance dropped and troubles began. After about two weeks of play each player received a check for $225. Our next check was for only $160. The third pay day netted a mere $77.

Owners of clubs in Venezuela and Puerto Rico heard about the drop in our finances and began luring away some of our players with promises of higher pay. I was surprised that so many of our players left. They were loyal as long as the pay had been decent in the Dominican Republic, but they couldn't resist the lure of money, and off they went. We held a meeting of the Federation and it was decided that those players who had jumped to other leagues would not be permitted to rejoin our league that winter. Sure enough, as soon as some of the teams had been eliminated from the pennant races in Venezuela and Puerto Rico, most of those players who had gone there tried to come back to our league. I was shocked when the president of our Federation, in violation of the rule we had passed, allowed those players to come back to our league for the remainder of the season. I knew that I was not the only player who resented this backing down and, as player representative for my team, I spoke out on the subject. My words went unnoticed and when I said that I would refuse to play any longer unless those players who had jumped were barred from the league, no one seemed to believe me. I felt it was a question of ethics and when I saw that the returning players were being welcomed back, I refused to play any more. This caused an uproar, but I was adamant and I did not rejoin my club. Making rules and then flaunting them has been one of the prime causes of turmoil in the Dominican Republic since its founding, and I felt that our Federation was making the same mistake.

It was time, I said, that Dominicans began to respect authority. Our Federation had a good chance to set an example for the other people in the Dominican Republic and I felt we had failed. At the time I stopped playing my team was in first place by about four games and I was leading the league with a .368 batting average. Because of my action, I was declared ineligible for the batting title. That was the least of my concerns. I was glad when I found that there were others who felt as I did and that before long newer and stronger rules had been adopted by the Federation.

I did a lot of fishing that winter and was more successful than ever. Many times I would go with a friend or two and we would return with 200 or 300 pounds of fish, most of which we gave away. My most constant fishing companion was a lad named Finfo. Finfo was about 19 years old and worked in a sand mine, while living in Haina. He has the biggest feet of anyone I have ever met. In fact, they resemble swim fins, hence his nickname. One day, Matty and Juan Marichal went fishing with us and it almost turned out to be a disaster. Matty got cramps in both legs and barely made it back to the boat. Juan, who had just finished his third straight season with more than 20 victories, had a close call, too. He was swimming under water when, suddenly, a spear from Finfo's powerful gun just missed him by inches.

One of the nicest things about that winter was that I had enough free time to attend church services regularly. Most of the year I live at a hectic pace, packing and unpacking my suitcase, flying from one city to another, trying to get proper rest. The major league schedule makes it difficult for me to get to all the church functions that I would like to. During 1963 and 1964 I received a number of letters from people who told me they felt it was wrong for me to play baseball on Sunday. This has always been a ticklish question, but I have resolved it as best I can.

It is my sincere belief that the Lord has established me in baseball for a reason and that if He wants me there, then I must comply with the demands of my profession. I feel that I would do more harm if I strutted around and insisted upon having Sundays off while the rest of my teammates had to play. My salary is based on my playing as many of the 162 games as the manager wants me to, not on how many games *I* wish to play. There is nothing that I enjoy more than having a Sunday off, a full day in which I can spend time with my wife and children and still be able to attend church services. My playing on Sundays, I believe, is as proper as a minister's preaching on Sundays. Ministers spend much of the week preparing for Sunday, not so that they can sit back and relax, but so that they can do the work they feel the Lord has called them to do. Preaching a sermon on Sunday is no easy task, but I am certain that the Lord does not frown upon the work these ministers perform on the Sabbath.

CHAPTER 15

GOD IS JUST SO GOOD AND THEN NO MORE

Shortly after arriving at the Braves' spring training headquarters in West Palm Beach, Florida in 1966, I had to return to the Dominican Republic. My parents had been notified by the Dominican government that unless back taxes on our property in Haina were paid in full the land would be confiscated. When I returned home for a few days I brought with me not only $6,700 to pay the taxes, but a large supply of vitamins for my wife, who was expecting our fourth child. Vitamins, so easy to get in the United States, were almost impossible to buy back home.

Once my financial affairs were straightened out, I took a day off to go fishing. While I was underwater I sighted a large fish, the size of which I could scarcely believe. I was about 40 feet down and had to maneuver carefully into position so that I could get a good shot with my spear gun. When I pulled the trigger the spear silently swooshed toward the fish. It struck hard. The fish swirled angrily, then fled. I thought that one shot might have finished him off, but he was too big and too tough to capture that easily. I lost sight of him, but after a few minutes of searching found him among some rocks and caves. He looked even bigger than before. It took another three shots to stop him. Then came the job of hauling him out of the water. When I finally beached him I was almost exhausted. He was a grouper and he was so large that I had him weighed. He came to 240 pounds. I have caught larger fish than that, but they were all sharks and I never bothered to weigh them. After stuffiing the grouper into the trunk of my car—there wasn't much room left—I drove to Haina to present the fish to friends and relatives to feast on. The next day I was on my way back to West Palm Beach.

There was an added aura of excitement about spring training in 1966, for everyone on the team was anxious about the shift of the team from Milwaukee to its new home in Atlanta. We got a preview of what life would be like in Atlanta when, near the end of spring training, we went there to play two exhibition games with the Dodgers. I don't know about my teammates, but I felt a bit of pressure. There had been a lot of bad feelings about the team leaving Milwaukee and members of the press were constantly trying to get comments from us on this touchy situation. Furthermore, there had been talk that colored players might not be received too well in Atlanta.

As it turned out, those two games in Atlanta did a lot to relieve my mind. Much ado was made about the poor attendance at our games. Cynics pointed out that the 25,000 people who came to the games indicated a lack of interest in baseball and, to substantiate their argument, they kept reminding us that 71,000 had showed up for a stock car race in Atlanta that same weekend. I could understand why not many people came to our games. For one thing, the temperature was in the 40s. For another, we had not yet established ourselves in Atlanta and had not had a chance to prove that we were worthy of affection. What relieved my apprehensions was the fact that wherever I went that weekend I found the Atlantans to be warm, receptive people. My personal contact with them—brief as it was—led me to believe that we wouldn't be regarded as outcasts for long. Getting on base six times in eight at bats and coming through with three doubles on Sunday also made me feel that Atlanta Stadium would be a good place to play in 1966.

All in all, I had a good spring. I led the team in hitting with a .349 average and was voted the most valuable player on the club during spring training.

Opening Day in Atlanta came on April 12th, and what a day it was. Some 250,000 people lined Peachtree Street as all the Braves rode by in open convertibles. Banners welcoming us to Atlanta were draped all over the city. The only thing that marred the day was our loss to the Pirates that night. Tony Cloninger struck out 12 men as he went the full 13 innings before losing on a two-run homer by Willie Stargell. Despite all the talk about lack of interest in Atlanta, 50,671 fans came to the game that night.

After the Pirates shut us out the next day, we left on a road trip. When we returned a week later we found out just how hardy and enthusiastic the Atlanta fans were. Almost 16,000 of them showed up for our first game against the Mets, even though it had rained for most of the day. I led off the bottom of the first inning with a single to left field that hit a puddle of water and sent up a showery spray. I remember Hank Aaron saying that, "You could have put little fish in those outfield puddles in the first inning and caught big ones in the second inning." Once I came in fast to try to scoop up a Met single in center field and came up with nothing but a glove full of water.

I had an excellent spring and I topped it off by going 5 for 5 in San Francisco on April 26th. My big day began when I hit the first pitch from Bob Bolin for a home run. Before the night was over, I had another homer, two doubles and a single and we had an 11-3 victory that moved us into second place. That was our 14th game of the season and I had hit in all of them, with my latest splurge raising my average to .393. I ran my hitting streak to 16 games before going 0 for 4 against Houston.

Right from the start of the season there was a strict enforcement of the major league rule against fraternization among opposing players on the field. The theory behind this rule is that the fans are not supposed to get any inkling that there might be friendships between players on different teams. Quite a few players were caught talking to opponents early in the year and each was assessed $25. I guess the cost of living in the majors has gone up considerably since that day a few years back when I was fined $10 for talking to Orlando Pena. This rule affects me more than most other players because I have brothers on two other teams, Matty having been traded from the Giants to the Pirates during the offseason. After not having seen Jesus for almost two months I had to be careful about even saying hello to him when we played the Giants for the first time in late April.

Another of the early-season problems was finding a place to live in Atlanta. By the time that Maria and the children arrived on April 29th, I had rented an apartment. It was a lovely place, but there were a lot of noisy neighbors who liked nothing better than to celebrate far into the night. I took my children out of school early because the national election was coming up soon in the Dominican Republic and this is always an occasion for riots and shooting. Agitators like to incite the children at election time and in the past a good many of them were innocent victims of the wild shooting that inevitably follows each rally or march.

Our club slumped badly after our good start and in early June we dropped into ninth place. Bobby Bragan summed up our situation in his own inimitable fashion by saying, "The hitters ain't hitting, the pitchers ain't pitching and the manager ain't managing." We reached one of our lowest points when we lost three straight to the Reds, who outhit us 39-16 and outscored us 23-6 in those games. During one stretch the Reds pitched more than the equivalent of a no-hitter against us, retiring 31 batters in a row. My average skidded more than 100 points in less than a month, falling to .284 on May 27th. Aaron, though not hitting for a high average, had 24 home runs before the end of June, thus matching a National League record. But Hank had troubles, too. Late in June he was struck out by what Bob Veale of the Pirates called his "integrated pitch." Explained Veale, "It caught both a little of the black and a little of the white of the plate." Aaron didn't appreciate the called third strike by Umpire

139

Tony Venzon and, as he headed for the dugout, he dropped his bat at home plate. Venzon kicked the bat toward Aaron, who kicked it right back. With a little soft-shoe thrown in here and there it would have been a pretty good act for television. As always, it was the umpire who had the punch line. We all sympathized with Aaron, not simply because he was tossed out of the game by Venzon but mainly because it was the first time Hank had been ejected after almost 2,100 games as a professional ballplayer. We lost that game 2-1 in 11 innings, provoking Bragan to comment that, "I don't understand it. We get good pitching and we lose 2-1, 3-2. We get good hitting and we lose 9-8, 7-6."

It was beginning to look like a bleak season in many ways. We had already hit our first snag in travelling when one of our flights to Atlanta had to be rerouted to Augusta, Georgia because of inclement weather. We spent all night and all morning waiting in the Augusta airport. Only the forceful efficiency of Donald Davidson, our travelling secretary, kept things from being worse than they were. Wielding his considerable influence, Davidson saw to it that the airport restaurant was opened at 5 a.m. so that we could get something to eat. He also got airlines officials to change their plans so that we could get out of Augusta ahead of schedule. As it was, we weren't able to leave until 7 a.m.

Davidson is as capable as he is short, and they don't come much shorter than Donald. who is 48⅞ inches small. During spring training in 1966 our team checked into a hotel in Tampa, Florida, but it wasn't long before players wound up in what must have been a banquet hall, which makes for an oversized bedroom but which also makes for worries that you'll wake up in the middle of dinner. All in all, the accommodations were far from satisfactory, so Davidson told off the manager of the hotel as only Davidson can tell off the manager of a hotel. Then he had to figure out where to take us.

He marched us through the streets of Tampa in search of a hotel. At the head of our procession was Donald, barely four feet tall, followed by such players as Hank Aaron, a six-footer, and Rico Carty, who is 6 foot 2. When Davidson finally found another hotel he marched us into the lobby and then, standing atop a borrowed portable typewriter, began telling the manager of the place who would be rooming together.

During that time—when the team was not winning, when our travel plans got all fouled up, when everyone seemed to be in a slump—an incident occurred which, now that I look back on it, surely made the difference between a so-so year and the good year I eventually had.

Someone said to me, in a moment of frustration, "God is just so good and then no more. He has been good to you, but one of these days He's going to stop being so good to you because *you* are no good."

That night in my room at the Roosevelt Hotel I prayed that God would help me show my friend that there is *no* limit to what God can, and will, do. I feel that what God enabled me to accomplish through the remainder of the season was His answer to my prayer.

Other troubles piled up. My children came down with bad colds. My wife was having a difficult pregnancy. When my mother and my sister Virginia came to Atlanta to help my wife late in June, they brought with them the news that my rowboat had been torn loose from its mooring during a storm and had been battered against the rocks. And my children were dropping their bubble gum all over the apartment. Ballplayers are inundated with bubble gum during the season and my three oldest children—Maria, Felipe and Jose—try their hardest to stay awake and wait until I come home after a night game so they can get some gum from me. If I forget to bring a handful of bubble gum home from the clubhouse, they get upset with me. My children are quite well behaved, but I have not been able to break them of their habit of taking bubble gum out of their mouth and putting it on the table, under the table, on the sofa, in their bed or just dropping it on the floor.

I had hoped that our fourth child would arrive during our homestand in late June. When it was evident that the child was going to be late, I had to make all the arrangements so that my wife would be taken care of while I was on the road. I had to make sure that there would be someone to drive her to the hospital, that the doctor would be informed and that all the little details would be attended to.

On July 2nd I called my wife from San Francisco and she assured me that all was well. My mind at ease, I went out that night and hit a 10th-inning home run to beat the Giants 3-1. That was my 18th homer of the season and, believe it or not, my first with a man on base. Little did I know that my wife had been fibbing to me about her condition. She had actually been feeling miserable when I had phoned but had not wanted to worry me. Later that night, at just about the time I was hitting my home run, she was on her way to the hospital. The next morning little Moises joined her. I must have been shaken up by the news. We had 20 hits on July 3rd, the day Moises was born, and I didn't have one of them. The way that Tony Cloninger hit that day, you would have thought he had just become the father of quadruplets. Cloninger became the first National Leaguer to hit two grand slam homers in one game and set a major league record for pitchers by driving in nine runs.

The next stop on our road trip was Houston and it was there that Donald Davidson handed me a plane ticket to St. Louis and told me that I had been selected for the All-Star team. I had played most of the season at first base after having started in the outfield and I did not get enough votes in the balloting among the players to earn a starting assignment in either spot. Walter Alston, the National League skipper, picked me as his No. 2 first baseman. At the time of the All-Star Game my batting average was up to .298, and I had 45 runs batted in and 20 homers. I didn't play in the game. The closest I came was to be in the on-deck circle as a pinch hitter when Maury Wills drove in the winning run for us in the bottom of the 10th inning.

Right after the All-Star Game I began slugging the ball and put together my second 16-game hitting streak of the season. During those 16 games I scored 19 runs, had 33 hits and batted .471, bringing my batting average up to .325. I was now third in the league batting race, 18 points behind Matty, who was driving pitchers to sleepless nights with his newfound ability to punch the ball to left field and to beat out chopped ground balls.

On the final day of my streak, I made one of the luckiest plays I've ever come up with at first base. The Giants had the bases loaded in the 10th inning when Ollie Brown hit a soft liner between first and second. I dived, hoping that I could knock the ball down and make a play somewhere. At first I didn't even realize I had caught the ball in the webbing of my glove but when I scrambled to my feet I saw that there was a chance to double the runner off third base. In my haste I made a bad throw and it took a leap by Third Baseman Eddie Mathews to catch the ball and keep the Giants from scoring. When I had made my catch, I had landed on my left elbow and slightly dislocated it, enough to make it hurt but not enough to make me leave the game. That injury was the prelude to what was to come.

The next day, July 31st, was one of the most hectic of the year. I had been trying for weeks to get my mother and sister booked on a flight to Santo Domingo but had been unable to get any tickets because of the airline strike. On July 30th I finally received confirmation for two tickets from Miami to Santo Domingo for the following day. It seems that two people, hearing that the strike was about to be settled, had decided to stay in the United States and tour the country. Unfortunately for them, the strike lasted almost another three weeks. I had to get up at 4 a.m. on July 31st so that I could get my mother and Virginia to the airport for a 5:45 plane. When I got back to the apartment I decided that I should call ahead to the Miami airport to make sure that someone from the airline would help my mother and sister, neither of whom spoke English. I wanted to be sure that they

"God Is Just So Good and Then No More"

got on their flight to Santo Domingo. That taken care of, I tried to go back to sleep. It was no use. Moises was serenading the neighborhood.

After having played a doubleheader the day before and getting so little sleep that night, I was weary by the time I got to the park for our afternoon game against the Giants. I had to get to the stadium earlier than usual because my elbow was badly swollen. The first pitch to me that day from Bob Bolin was in close. My reflexes must have been slow, because, instead of ducking out of the way of the ball, I stuck my left arm up to protect my face. It felt as though someone had skewered me when the fastball hit my throbbing left elbow. I was a little angry about having been hit and I no sooner got to first base than I decided to steal second. The throw from Giant Catcher Ozzie Virgil was high and Second Baseman Hal Lanier had to leap to catch it. I slid in head first and when Lanier came down he landed on my right hand, gouging my thumb with his spikes. In two of my last three at bats that day I hit the ball well, but Shortstop Tito Fuentes picked off a line drive I thought might have gone through and Willie Mays made a running catch in left center on the last ball I hit. Both of those drives might well have been hits had my elbow not been hurting so much that I couldn't pull the ball too well.

My hitting streak hadn't helped win many games and as August turned the corner we were tied for eighth place, 12½ games from the top. One of our most dramatic victories of the season came on August 8th, in a game with Los Angeles that started like a runaway when we scored five runs in the first inning. The Dodgers pecked away at our lead, however, tied the score at 6-6 in the eighth and then went in front with three runs in the top of the ninth. There had already been two dozen hits in the game, but we added another half dozen in the bottom of the ninth, scored four times and won 10-9. The victory was credited to Relief Pitcher Phil Niekro, who came on in the ninth and threw just two pitches in getting the final Dodger out. After the game Niekro said that two had become his lucky number in recent days. It seems that over the weekend just prior to the game he had been married, not once, but twice. After being pronounced man and wife on Saturday, he got a call from the minister, who said that he had left something out of the ceremony. So Phil and his bride went to the minister's home on Sunday and were married again.

There was something significant for me in that game, too. I had come to bat in the midst of our ninth-inning rally and had grounded the ball weakly to second. It took every ounce of hustle I could muster to beat out that little nubber for a single that kept us going. I've always tried to be a hustling ballplayer but since I had prayed for

143

the Lord to help me after that problem in early June, I found that I was trying harder than ever. I think if someone had told me to try harder yet, I would have told them, "I can't. I'm giving the game everything I've got." Some things are unexplainable, yet it seemed that since my plea to the Lord for help, I had been hustling even more. One thing I do know is that Colossians 3:23 really meant something to me now:

"And whatsoever ye do, do it heartily, as to the Lord,
and not unto men. . . . "

I found that I had reached a new plateau, that I was no longer striving to get hits and to make fielding plays only for my own good and for the good of the team. Now exerting myself "as unto the Lord, and not unto men," it seemed that He was supplying me with abilities that had heretofore been out of my reach. A number of people, both in sports and in other areas of work, have told me that they have experienced much the same thing. They told me that they found that the more they yielded themselves to God the more He supplied their needs and helped them accomplish the very same thing they had unsuccessfully been trying to do for years. I, too, believe that the Lord had extended a hand to me and I thanked Him for His help, which is, both literally and figuratively, above all.

CHAPTER 16

NO END

It was 7:40 in the morning on the day after we had defeated the Dodgers 10-9. As Billy Hitchcock, one of the coaches on the Braves, reached for the jangling telephone he was still half asleep. He woke up fast. Billy, who had managed the Baltimore Orioles a few years earlier, had just received word that he was replacing Bobby Bragan as the manager of our club. I heard the news that morning on the radio. If Bragan had to go, I was glad to see Hitchcock replace him. Hitchcock, a quiet man who seemed to have been born with a pipe in his mouth, was well respected by all the players.

I was sorry to see Bragan leave, though. He was a fine man, a humorous man, a man who had enough confidence in me to bat me anywhere in the lineup and play me at just about any infield or outfield position. His faith in my ability gave me added confidence, and that was comforting at age 31. Baseball is 50 per cent confidence; if you feel you can do the job, that's half the fight; if you feel you can't do it, you're not going to.

When Hitchcock took over the club we were mired in seventh place and were seven games under .500. Before his first game as manager, he held a clubhouse meeting. He began by saying, "I don't want to make a long speech." He told us he would be the manager for the rest of the season and that he would not make many changes in the handling of the team. Hitchcock made just two changes at first. He told Eddie Mathews, who had played more than 2,000 games as a Brave but who had spent a lot of time on the bench recently, that he was his third baseman. Hitchcock also moved me back to the leadoff spot because, as he put it, "After you hit in the first inning the score may be 1-0."

Sandy Koufax of the Dodgers pitched against us that day and when I faced him in the first inning the count went to 3 and 2. I hit his next pitch over the left field fence and, just like Hitchcock said, the score was 1-0. That's the way the score remained until Jim Lefebvre led off the Dodger eighth with a home run, the first hit allowed by Denny Lemaster. Mathews came to bat in the ninth with the score still 1-1. Koufax had struck him out three times that day, getting him with high fastballs. Mathews, who was 34 at the time, knew he should have either laid off those pitches or, if he *was* going to swing at them, should have taken a full cut at the ball. Disgusted with himself, Eddie turned to Dodger Catcher John Roseboro when he came up in the ninth and said, "Don't ever grow old." Within a minute, Mathews was gamboling around the bases as though he were a young 24 and the whole team greeted him when he crossed home plate after his home run.

Hitchcock, whose only moves had both paid off, could have spouted off to the press, but instead gave the credit to the players. Billy also called one of the shortest clubhouse meetings on record. All he had to say was, "Thanks men. Let's keep playing like that." We appreciated both his brevity and his sincerity. And we appreciated what the fans did that night. There were 52,270 at the game—a record for Atlanta Stadium—and, despite a two-hour-and-five-minute rain delay in the fourth inning, very few of them left. When the umpires said that it was all right to resume play, it was thrilling to see all those fans still there. It's uncomfortable to have to sit around on a rainy day and we knew that those who did were telling us by their very presence that we were not regarded as strangers or carpetbaggers.

Don Drysdale was the starting pitcher for the Dodgers in our second game under Hitchcock and for the second day in a row I led off the first inning with a home run, my 25th of the season. We won that game 3-1, our third straight victory over Los Angeles. Later in the month, though, we lost three in a row to the Dodgers and I was to blame for the last of those losses. I made an error in the 11th inning that led to the run that beat us. Even though I had cost us the game, I got a favorable review the next day from Furman Bisher, the sports editor of *The Atlanta Journal.* Bisher wrote, "Alou came into the game with a sore throat. But he insisted on playing and play he did. . . . Forgive Alou his boot. If it hadn't been for a fantastic catch he made on Ron Fairly's line drive with speedy Willie Davis on first in the ninth, the game would have already been over, anyway. He doubled up Davis, ending the inning."

Atlanta sportswriters—including Jesse Outlar, sports editor of *The Atlanta Constitution,* and his No. 1 baseball writer, Wilt Browning, as well as Wayne Minchew of *The Constitution*—were kind to me all year. I have been fortunate in never having been badly misquoted, but there have been instances when writers have irked me. The worst sportswriters anywhere, I believe, are in the Dominican Republic. Some don't even come to the games, preferring to listen to the radio broadcasts. Much the same is true about those writers who cover news for the papers back home. I know that my people learn most of what they know about politics, economics and society in the Dominican Republic from reading what foreign authors have to say.

American sportswriters are much better. I have read only two stories that have upset me to any degree since I reached the major leagues. The first was when a San Francisco writer referred to me as a nice person but a lousy player. That didn't bother me nearly as much as what was written about me in one of those cheap once-a-year baseball magazines that are written by opinionated and usually uninformed men. This particular issue was one I picked up when I returned to spring training after my few days at home to pay off taxes. It went on and on about how old I was—it said I was 34 or 36, I believe, when actually I was 30—and that I was more of a liability than an asset to the team. As much as I didn't want to put any stock in that magazine, it hurt me to think that I was held in such low regard and such trash could be printed. It made me angry, but there wasn't anything I could do except go out and prove on the field that I was going to help the club.

As for sports announcers, just a few comments. Being a baseball announcer is demanding, for the season lasts from March through September and is full of road trips, odd hours and foul weather—just as it is for the players. Most announcers do a good job in spite of these difficulties. An announcer's slightest slip-up on the air is picked up by some, if not all, of his listeners, who often mimic or downgrade him. Having made a few errors of my own on the playing field, I would like to think that all of us—players and fans alike—could be as kind to announcers when they goof as Furman Bisher, Jesse Outlar, and other Atlanta writers were to me all year.

I have just one request to make of announcers and that is that they check with players who have unusual names on how those names should be pronounced. There are many hard-to-pronounce names and I am sure that any ballplayer would be happy to clarify his for any announcer. It would be even simpler if announcers compiled a book giving the correct pronunciation of players' names, a method that would guarantee that Zoilo Versalles' name would not be pronounced Ver-sales by one announcer, Ver-sigh-ees by another and Ver-sol-iss by a third.

The announcers for the Braves—Milo Hamilton, Larry Munson and Ernie Johnson—did a fine job in 1966. They had much to do with getting the fans to accept us so completely. Hamilton's grandest moment came on Banner Day, an event he had been plugging on the air for weeks. When the day turned up rainy and miserable, Banner Day seemed doomed. There was an excellent crowd, though, many of them carrying banners using the nicknames and phrases coined by Hamilton, who, among other things, gave Hank Aaron a monicker that finally stuck: The Hammer.

In addition to what Bisher wrote, another unexpectedly kind remark was made about me late in the season by Paul Richards, who had recently joined the Braves' front office. Said Richards, "Felipe is the greatest ballplayer in the world." This comment was made after a seven-game stretch in which I had had 19 hits, including four doubles, a triple and a homer, and had produced 13 runs. That was quite a tribute, coming from Richards, but I wasn't about to believe it anymore than he was. Why he made such a statement I don't know. I do know, however, that both of us realize there are other players who are better than I am.

I have found that as soon as I start to take myself too seriously something happens that brings my perspective into line. There are always little reminders of just how fallible I am. I recall sliding into second base on the final play of a game against the Cubs in August. As I headed for the clubhouse I heard a number of people calling my name. Any thoughts about how popular I had suddenly become were dispelled when I looked down and noticed that the whole left inside leg of my uniform had been ripped open.

There have been other sobering moments.

When I was a frisky teenager just beginning to think that I was a pretty good player, I learned my first lesson. It was while I was in Mexico for the Central-American Games that a ball hit me right on top of the head. For weeks thereafter I had bad headaches, not to mention a somewhat bruised ego.

My worst experience came while I was still with the Giants. We were playing the Reds and when we went into the bottom of the ninth inning with a one-run lead to protect, I was put into the outfield in place of Leon Wagner. Just about the time I began to think that it was nice to get off the bench and that I could help our team, a long fly ball was hit my way by Whitey Lockman. I caught the ball easily—then dropped it! The Cincinnati runner on second base scored the tying run on a ball that I should have caught for the final out of the day. Lockman wound up on second on my error and scored the winning run when the next player singled. I still get chills when I think about that game and I remember how awful I felt. There was a feeling of being squeezed into a corner with nowhere to go and as I left the field I had an urge to climb over the center field wall and flee. It's a terrible sensation to walk into your clubhouse after having given away a game like that. Certainly, I was charged with an error that day, but it was the pitcher who was given the loss and because of me he had to wear the infamous L after his name in the boxscore. I was so upset that night that I couldn't sleep. Now, if I made such an error I don't think I would feel quite the same way. By that I mean I would be just as sorry for my team and the pitcher, but I wouldn't let it affect me as deeply because I know that if I did, it would hurt my play the next day or two and, therefore, would harm my club even further.

Shortly after Hitchcock became manager he decided to move all the coaches to the same side of the clubhouse where he was now located. My locker was on that side, so he came to me and said, "Felipe, I know you're having a good year and I don't know whether you want to give up your locker or not. Some players are superstitious about that sort of thing." I told him I would gladly move to the other side of the clubhouse and I had no sooner made the shift than one of the local sportswriters came to me somewhat aghast and said, "How can someone like you, who's already got more than 160 hits, switch lockers at a time like this?"

"Don't worry," I told him. "I never did get a hit in that old locker; they've all been on the field." After suiting up in my new locker, I got two hits that day on the field.

The locker I had taken over had belonged to Grover Resinger, a coach who had resigned when Bragan was fired. Earlier in the season Resinger's locker had become the focal point of a prank by Catcher Joe Torre, one of the team's leading jokers. To appreciate the gag, you must realize that Resinger was an intense man who had waited around in the back corridors of baseball's minor leagues for more than 20 years before Bragan brought him up as a coach in 1966. While Resinger was on the field during pregame warmups one day, Torre was in the clubhouse packing all of Grover's gear into suitcases. When Resinger came back to the clubhouse he found that his locker was empty and that the name of Bill Adair, a manager in the Atlanta farm system, had been inserted on the top of the locker where his name had been. Resinger was genuinely shaken.

Not long after moving into my new locker I received a package containing a skin-diving outfit, my payment from Topps for permitting them to use my picture with their bubble gum. Each player who signs with Topps is paid either $125 in cash or the equivalent from their gift catalogue. Torre was intrigued by the scuba equipment and often put on the whole outfit and stalked around the clubhouse. I was sure that one day before the end of the season Torre was going to go right on the field wearing the black rubber suit, fins and goggles.

My move to the other side of the clubhouse didn't hurt my hitting and on the 1st of September I raised my average to .330 and moved into second place among the league's top hitters. Ten points in front of me was Matty, who was leading the majors in hitting. After a dismal start, Jesus was also doing well. With his average hovering around .200, Jesus had been sent down to Phoenix for two weeks in

June. He had seven hits in his first 13 at bats after being recalled by the Giants and in August helped keep the Giant pennant hopes flickering as he batted .369.

There were a number of reasons why I was hitting better than ever, none of them more vital, however, than the aggressive attitude I had assumed at the plate. I was letting the pitcher know that I was ready to hit against him and that I didn't care who he was, what his reputation was or whether he was a righthander or a lefthander. There were other reasons for my improvement, too. In 1965 I had hit too many fly balls for long outs. Now I was hitting more on top of the ball, swinging down so that I would hit more line drives, and ground balls. It seems illogical to swing down and hit line drives, but this is the way it is done and it takes discipline to curb the natural tendency to swing up on a ball. I was hit by a dozen pitches in 1966—making me the third most-bruised player in the league—but I knew that if I gave in to the "jammer" and backed off from the plate the pitchers would be able to set me up the way they used to.

Hitting looks very simple to most people. At times it seems simple to me also. Once I get into the batter's box, though, and the interplay, psychology and warfare between pitcher and batter begins, I remember very quickly how difficult hitting really is. The pitcher has a number of plusses in his favor. He has a weapon of sorts in his hand, a baseball that he can throw at 80 or more miles an hour over a distance of only 60 feet and six inches. That gives the hitter only a fraction of a second to make up his mind whether to hit, take or duck. A pitcher is generally better rested than a batter, having had the advantage of a few days off between pitching assignments—unless he is a busy reliefer. It is impossible for a hitter to concentrate fully on every pitch thrown to him. Using myself as an example, I can estimate that in the slightly more than 700 times I batted in 1966 I saw an average of four pitches per bat, or a total of 2,800 pitches.

In 1966 I learned how to hustle at the plate. By that I mean that I was able to force myself to be more alert for each pitch than in past years. Using a heavier bat helped, too. In 1965, because of my leg operation the year before, I started using a lighter bat so that I could swing harder and get more power from my arms. My bat was a little quicker perhaps, but I couldn't get any sting with the light bat and couldn't get any distance on my hits. Late in 1965 I gave up on my light bat (35 inches, 33 ounces) in favor of a heavier one (36 inches, 36 ounces). Some fans think players are kidding when they make such changes, but even a slight one such as that has its effect.

Another minute alteration that was of value was that I opened my stance just a trifle so that I wouldn't have to put as much weight on my right leg, which was not as strong since the operation. I found that I was strong enough to hit the ball out of any park in any direction, so I cut down on trying to pull the ball and merely tried to hit the ball where it was pitched—outside pitches to right field, inside pitches to left.

Precisely how much each of these little items contributed to my hitting is impossible to judge. One thing I do know, though, is that my aggressiveness triggered my batting resurgence and that this new attitude was, in turn, made possible by my mental attitude. In 1966 my mind was more at ease than ever because I had let the Lord take over more of my life than ever. He was accomplishing that which I could not.

The higher my average went, the more I found that pitchers changed their patterns of pitching to me. At the start of the season they all tried to jam me. When I started hitting those inside pitches into the left field seats, the pitchers began feeding me outside deliveries. This cut down my home run production slightly, but helped build my average higher as I hit more singles to right and center.

When pitchers get frustrated they are apt to resort to a few tricks to try to get the batter out. Believe me, they are not afraid to throw the spitball, even though it is illegal. The whole spitball situation has become one of the biggest shams in baseball. There is a baseball rule that says that no foreign substance can be applied to the ball. Spit is regarded as a foreign substance, yet umpires have *never* pointed a finger at a pitcher for throwing a spitter. Ask any batter, and he will tell you that the spitter is commonplace. Add to that the confessions of several pitchers who have admitted throwing the spitter and you have evidence that undeniably proves that the spitball flourishes today. I can't understand how the same umpires, who are so eagle-eyed about spotting players who fraternize on the field, can be so unobservant when it comes to the spitball. On the other hand, I sympathize with the umpires, who have enough to do without trying to enforce ambiguous rules concerning the spitball.

The permissiveness has reached the stage where more and more pitchers are not afraid to use the spitter. You can watch them practice with it openly on the sidelines or in the bullpen. Gaylord Perry of the Giants came up with a good spitter in 1966 and his 21 victories will surely inspire other pitchers to work harder on their spitters. Few pitchers, though, have as good an arm as Perry, who sets up his wetball with an excellent fastball and slider. Having a spitter does not mean a pitcher will be a winner—especially when he is pitted against another spitballer—but it gives him an edge that, according to the rules, is illegal.

Aside from Perry, some of the better spitball pitchers in the National League are Don Drysdale and Phil Regan of the Dodgers, and Bob Shaw and Jack Hamilton of the Mets. Some people say that as long as pitchers can get away with what they are doing, more power to them. I say that a game that prides itself on its integrity and is trying to sell itself as the symbol of American honesty is making a farce out of itself on this issue. I think that a courageous crackdown on the spitter by the Commissioner of Baseball and/or the league presidents would earn more respect for the game than anything else. I know, for example, that some pitchers have so little respect for the nonexistent ban on the spitball that they openly use slippery elm, among other things. Slippery elm is used to make a person salivate heavily. It has been declared illegal, yet a surprising number of pitchers go out to the mound with slippery elm in their mouth.

There is no doubt that the spitter makes it harder to get hits.

Another thing that cut my average was that I batted leadoff for much of the year. This is an added burden, particularly when on the road, for it means that you start the game cold, without the benefit of having been in the field for the first half inning. One of the bad things about being the leadoff batter is that you often get one more at bats than most other players and, when you are having a poor day at the plate it can mean going 0 for 5 instead of 0 for 4. Once I began hitting the ball well, pitchers concentrated harder on getting me out, frequently giving me their best pitch on their first delivery.

A good many players, including myself, prefer to play night games. I like playing at night even more now that I am in Atlanta, where the evenings rarely get cold enough to be bothersome. My main reason for preferring nighttime competition is that there is uniformity in the playing conditions; the ball looks white from the first inning through the last, whereas during the day you often cannot get a true look at the ball because of cloud conditions, the glare of the sun or oncoming darkness.

It took every bit of aggressiveness, determination and concentration I had to bring my average up from .284 on May 27th to well over .300. A little luck here and there didn't hurt, either. There was a game back in July when Dodger Catcher John Roseboro dropped a pop-up I had hit. Given another chance, I stepped up again and hit a home run off Sandy Koufax. Later in the game I hit a two-run homer off Koufax and we beat him 5-2. At one time during the season I had four home runs off Koufax in six at bats.

Not all my luck was good, though. Early in September I made a risky play at first base in an attempt to keep a bad throw from bouncing past me. I didn't have much time to think about whether to make the play or not, but I know I was motivated by the thought that I must always try my hardest. In trying my hardest, I kept the ball from skipping past me but wound up having my glove hand badly slashed by Gene Alley of the Pirates. His spikes almost tore the thumb off my glove and also gashed my hand. When I looked down and saw the shredded glove and the blood running down my wrist, I figured I was through for the year. It wasn't as bad an injury as I feared and a day or so later I got my 200th hit of the season, a single off Al McBean of the Pirates. During the next ten days I batted .364 and brought my average up to .331. Then, on September 18th, the first pitch from Cincinnati Pitcher Sammy Ellis was behind my head. I put up my left hand to protect my face and the ball hit my hand and I suffered a hairline fracture. It was eight days before I was back in the lineup and in the few remaining games I hit just .252. Still, 1966 was the best season of my career. Matty led the majors in hitting with a .342 average and I was second at .327. I also drove in 74 runs and hit 31 homers, and I finished fifth in the voting for The Most Valuable Player award in the National League. What pleased me as much as anything, though, was that our club won 32 of 51 games under Hitchcock and finished in fifth place, six games over .500.

After a three-week rest at home following the end of the 1966 National League season, I was back playing baseball again in the Dominican League. On Opening Day, Matty, Jesus and I were the first three batters for our Escogido team. Matty singled, then stole second. Jesus hit back to the pitcher, who caught Matty in a rundown between second and third. Matty slid back to second safely, then scrambled to his feet and raced to third, beating the throw to the catcher, who was covering the base. When Matty noticed that there was no one covering home, he got up again and stole home. During the frantic running around, Jesus stole second. I followed with a single that scored Jesus and on the throw to the plate I took second, from where I scored on two infield outs. People in Santo Domingo were saying, "The telephone is working again."

Epilogue

We have a couple of days off each week during the winter season and I spend some of my free time fishing, some of it visiting friends and relatives, some of it thinking. It is impossible not to see the poverty of the people in my country. I see the men who sell peanuts for a living, just as they have been doing all their life. There are still the young men arguing, fighting for causes they don't even understand. I see many Felipe Alous working in the fields, running barefoot, climbing coconut trees. Everywhere people are struggling for food, for the tiniest sliver of happiness.

I think about a rookie I heard of in the American League in 1966, a boy named George Scott of the Red Sox, who as a youngster had picked cotton in the Mississippi fields until his hands bled but who wouldn't wear gloves because they cut down on the work he could do and, therefore, the money he would earn. And I think about Cal McLish, who used to pitch in the National League until not long ago. Most people only knew him because he had the longest name in the big leagues—Calvin Coolidge Julius Caeser Tuskahoma McLish. He knew squalor in rural Oklahoma, was born in a barn, spent part of his childhood living in a dugout-cave. His father was sick, his mother worked in a burlap bag factory and there was so little to hope for. But Cal McLish was a good pitcher and baseball gave him a home. There have been many other George Scotts and Cal McLishes before and there will be others to come.

Down by the sea I watch the waves spank the shore. I see Matty running home with the crab dangling from his arm, Jesus snitching food from the kitchen, my father going off to work, my mother crying about the $10 bill we lost. There is Navarro telling me to be patient, Kerr urging me not to give up, Roque reaching out to help, Worthington answering my questions. So many people who have extended their hands to help. I see, too, that there is, above all, the helping hand of the Lord, who reaches out to help all men and who took me through troubled waters and showed me that there is *no* end to how good He is.